S0-DOQ-435

stamping

for the home

stamping

✳

for the home

contemporary designs to transform
floors, walls, and soft furnishings

STEWART and SALLY WALTON

PHOTOGRAPHY BY GRAHAM RAE

LORENZ BOOKS

FOR ROBIN BICKNELL
1947 – 1995

This edition published by Lorenz Books in 2001
© Anness Publishing 1995, 2001

Lorenz Books is an imprint of Anness Publishing Limited
Hermes House, 88–89 Blackfriars Road, London SE1 8HA
www.lorenzbooks.com

Published in the USA by Lorenz Books, Anness Publishing Inc.
27 West 20th Street, New York, NY 10011

This edition distributed in Canada by Raincoast Books
9050 Shaughnessy Street, Vancouver, British Columbia V6P 6E5

All rights reserved. No part of this publication may be reproduced, stored in a retrieval system,
or transmitted in any way or by any means, electronic, mechanical, photocopying, recording or
otherwise, without the prior written permission of the copyright holder.

A CIP catalogue record for this book is available from the British Library.

Publisher: *Joanna Lorenz*   Project editor: *Lindsay Porter*
Photographer: *Graham Rae*   Designer: *Bobbie Colgate Stone*
Cover Design: *D.W. Design*   Stylist: *Diana Civil*

The authors would like to thank Sacha Cohen, Sarah Pullin and Nigel Goldsmith for their energy
and enthusiasm in the studio.

Previously published as *Stamp Style*

10 9 8 7 6 5 4 3 2 1

NOTE: PVA glue is known in the USA as white glue. Emulsion paint is also known as latex paint.

CONTENTS

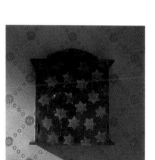

$\mathscr{I}$NTRODUCTION

STAMPING is one of the most instant and versatile forms of decorating available. Unbelievably simple yet stunningly effective, stamped designs can be used to brighten up anything from an entire wall to a sheet of giftwrap. Use them to create a theme for a whole room or to provide an eye-catching focal point. To get started, all you need is a stamp, a brush or roller and paint, or an inkpad. Application is trouble free, so let your imagination run riot and create beautifully patterned walls and fabrics in no time.

In order to understand the possibilities of stamp-making and printing, it helps first to take a look at the traditional "office" rubber stamp. It consists of a rubber "die" - the cut-out design - mounted on a thin bed of foam and then a wooden back with a handle. The rubber picks up ink from a stamp pad, holds it and then releases it on to paper under a light pressure. The foam mounting acts as a shock absorber, so the rubber can take the pressure without sustaining any damage. Rubber stamps like this stand up to years of constant use, especially when used with indelible ink which has a protective quality.

The stamps used for home decorating need some of the qualities described above, but not all are strictly necessary. It is highly unlikely that anyone would want to keep a decorating stamp in constant use, so it is preferable and much cheaper to use medium- or high-density foam sponge for projects like patterned walls or furniture. Stamps can also be made from wood, linoleum or string - almost any material that will hold colour and release it. The colour can be ink or nearly any kind of paint.

This chapter describes some of the stamp-making options and design possibilities. The projects have step-by-step photographs as a guide for each stage, and there are pattern templates to trace at the end of the book.

CREATING STAMPS

WOOD AND LINO STAMPS

Stamped prints were first made with carved wooden blocks. Indian textiles are still produced by hand in this way and it has recently become possible to buy traditional carved printing blocks.

Designs are cut in outline and the backgrounds are scooped out to leave the pattern shapes standing proud of the surface. Ink is applied, either by dipping the block or rolling colour on to the surface. The design is stamped and appears in reverse. The craft of making wooden printing blocks takes time to learn: you need special tools that are razor sharp, and an understanding about cutting with or against the grain. Practise on a bonded wood like marine plywood, which is relatively easy to carve.

Lino blocks are available from art and craft suppliers and usually come ready mounted in a range of sizes. Lino is a natural material made from ground cork and linseed oil on a webbed string backing. It is cut in the same way as wood, but has a less resistant texture and no grain to contend with, so is simple to cut.

To make a lino stamp you will need to trace a design and reverse the tracing before transferring it to the lino; this way you will print the design the right way around. Fill in all the background areas with a permanent marker pen: these are the parts to be scooped out, leaving the design proud of the surface. You will need a minimum of three tools – a scalpel, a "V"-shaped gouge and a scoop. All the tools should be kept as sharp as possible to make cutting easier and safer. Lino is easiest to cut when slightly warm, so place the block on a radiator for ten minutes before cutting. Hold the block with your spare hand behind your cutting hand, then if the tool slips you will not hurt yourself.

FOAM STAMPS

Different types of foam are characterized by their density. The main types used for stamp-making in this book are: high-density foam, such as upholstery foam; medium-density sponge, such as a kitchen sponge; and low-density sponge, such as a bath sponge. The different densities of foam are each suited to a particular kind of project; on the whole, medium- or low-density sponges are best for bold solid shapes, and high-density foam for fine details. Polystyrene foam can also be used but must be mounted on to hardboard. When the glue has dried, the polystyrene can be cut through to

 Create the effect of wood blocks (top) with handmade lino cuts (bottom).

There are two methods of creating your own rubber stamps. The first is to design on paper and then have a rubber-stamp company make one for you. This is worth doing if you intend to make good use of the stamp, and not just use it for a small, one-off project. Custom-made stamps are quite expensive to produce, so unless money is no object you may like to consider a second option. You can also make stamps by carving your design into an ordinary eraser. Many erasers are now made of a plastic compound instead of actual rubber, but the surface is smooth and easy to cut into. Two projects in this book, the tea service and personalized stationery, show you how to transfer and cut a pattern, and then print from a homemade rubber stamp.

▲ *Homemade stamps cut from high- and medium-density foam.*

▼ *Commercial rubber stamps are available in designs to suit all tastes.*

the board and the background can be lifted, leaving the design as a stamp.

To make a sponge stamp, first trace your chosen design then lightly spray the back of the pattern with adhesive, which will make it tacky but removable. Stick the pattern on to the foam and use a sharp scalpel to cut around the shape. Remove any background by cutting across to meet the outlines. If you are using medium- or low-density sponge, part it after the initial outline cut, then cut right through to the other side. High-density foam can be cut into and carved out in finer detail, it is also less absorbent, so you get a smoother, less textured print. If you are stamping over a large area, it is easier to mount the foam on to a

hardboard base and use wood glue to attach a small wooden door knob to the back, as a handle.

RUBBER STAMPS

Rubber stamps have come out of the office and playroom and emerged as remarkable interior decorating tools. Shops have sprung up dealing exclusively in an incredible range of stamp designs and the mail-order selections are astounding. The advantage of these pre-cut stamps is that you are instantly ready to transform fabric, furniture, even walls – and there can be no quicker way to add pattern to a surface. However, rubber stamps are most suited to small projects that require fine detail.

CREATING STAMPS

JACOBEAN POLYSTYRENE FLOWER

Polystyrene is easy to cut and gives good, clean edges. Always mount the polystyrene on hardboard before you cut your pattern.

YOU WILL NEED
- *sheet of polystyrene foam, approximately 1cm/½in thick*
- *piece of hardboard, the same size as the polystyrene*
- *wood glue or PVA glue*
- *felt-tipped pen*
- *scalpel*

1 Stick the sheet of polystyrene and hardboard backing together with wood glue or PVA glue.

2 Without waiting for the glue to set, draw the design using a felt-tipped pen. Remember that the pattern will reverse when printed.

3 Cut around the outline of the design using a scalpel. If this is done before the glue has set, these pieces will pull away easily.

4 Cut the edging details, removing unwanted pieces as you go.

5 Make shallow, angular cuts and scoop out the pattern details of the design. Use a new blade for this so that the cuts are sharp and you do not accidentally lift adjoining particles that have been only partially separated.

GEOMETRIC BORDER DESIGN

This border stamp is made from high-density foam. A good quality upholstery foam is recommended. The piece used here was sold by a camping supply shop for use as a portable, compact mattress.

YOU WILL NEED
- ♦ *wood glue or PVA glue*
- ♦ *high-density foam, such as upholstery foam, cut to the size of your design*
- ♦ *hardboard, cut to the same size*
- ♦ *felt-tipped pen*
- ♦ *ruler*
- ♦ *scalpel*
- ♦ *wooden block, for the handle*

1 Stick the foam on to the hardboard by applying wood glue or PVA glue to the rough side.

2 Without waiting for the glue to set, draw the pattern on to the foam using a felt-tipped pen and ruler. Use a scalpel to outline the sections to be cut away, then lift them out. If the glue is still tacky, this will be much easier.

3 Finally, using wood glue or PVA glue, stick the wooden block in the middle of the stamp back, to act as a handle. Allow to dry thoroughly.

SQUIGGLE FOAM STAMP

Foam comes in all shapes, sizes and densities. Make a visit to a specialist foam dealer, as inspiration for new ideas often springs from the discovery of new materials. Here is an idea for making a squiggle stamp in an original way.

YOU WILL NEED
- ♦ *masking tape*
- ♦ *length of cylindrical foam, about 2cm/¾in in diameter*
- ♦ *wood glue or PVA glue*
- ♦ *hardboard*

1 Lay out a length of masking tape, sticky side up. Twist the foam into a squiggle shape, pressing it on to the middle section of the tape.

2 Apply wood glue or PVA glue to the untaped side of the foam and turn it face-down on to the hardboard. Fold the tape ends under the hardboard to hold the foam in place while the glue sets. When dry, peel off the masking tape.

FLORAL LINOCUT

Cutting lino is a simple technique to master. You will be delighted with the intricacy of the motifs you can create using this medium.

YOU WILL NEED
- *tracing paper*
- *pencil*
- *sheet of transfer paper*
- *lino block*
- *masking tape*
- *scalpel*
- *lino-cutting tools: a "V"-shaped gouge and a "U"-shaped scoop*

1 Make a tracing of your chosen motif, the same size as the lino block. Slip a sheet of transfer paper (chalky side down) between the tracing and the lino, then tape the edges with masking tape.

2 Draw over the pattern lines with a sharp pencil. The tracing will appear on the lino block.

3 Remove the paper and cut around the outline with a scalpel. Cut any fine detail or straight lines by making shallow, angular cuts from each side, then scoop out the "V"-shaped sections.

4 Cut the rest of the pattern using the lino tools - the scoop for removing large areas of background, and the gouge for cutting the finer curves and pattern details. Hold the lino down firmly, with your spare hand placed behind your cutting hand to avoid accidents.

POTATO PRINT SUNBURST

Most of us learn the technique of
using potatoes for printing as very
young schoolchildren. Potato prints
are amazingly effective, and should not
be overlooked by adults.

YOU WILL NEED
- ♦ *medium-sized raw potato*
- ♦ *sharp kitchen knife*
- ♦ *fine felt-tipped pen*
- ♦ *scalpel*

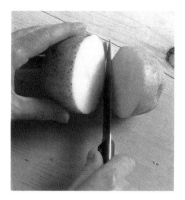

1 Use a kitchen knife to make a single
cut right through the potato. This will
give the smoothest surface.

2 Draw the motif on to the potato
with a fine felt-tipped pen.
Remember that motifs reverse when
stamped, although with the sunburst
motif used here it will make no
difference.

3 Use a scalpel to cut the outline,
then undercut and scoop out the
background. Potato stamps will not
last longer than a few hours before
they deteriorate, so keep a tracing of
your motif if your project cannot be
completed in one go. The design can
then be re-cut using a fresh potato.

APPLICATION TECHNIQUES

In the world of stamping, the coating of a stamp with colour is always known as inking, regardless of the substance applied. There are no hard and fast rules about what can or cannot be used - any substance that coats a stamp and is then released on to a surface when stamped, will be suitable.

Stamp inkpads come in a wide range of shapes, sizes and colours. Some contain permanent ink and others are water-based and washable.

Paints can be applied with brushes or rollers, or spread on to a flat surface and the stamp dipped into them. Experiment with different paints and inks and always test stamp on scrap paper first before starting a project.

USING A BRUSH

This is a way of applying thick water-based paint such as emulsion or artist's acrylic. One big advantage here is that you can use several colours on one stamp in a very controlled way. This would not be possible if you were inverting the stamp on an inkpad.

USING A ROLLER

Place a blob of paint on one side of a flat plate and run a small rubber roller through it several times until it is covered evenly with colour. Run the roller over the rubber stamp to transfer the paint. Make a test print on paper, as this method sometimes overloads the stamp with paint.

USING AN INKPAD

Simply press the rubber stamp lightly on to the surface of the stamp inkpad. Check that the stamp is evenly coated, then make your print. It is difficult to overload the stamp using this method.

DIPPING SPONGE STAMPS

Spread an even coating of paint on to a flat plate and simply dip the sponge stamp into it. Check that the stamp is evenly coated, then make a test print on scrap paper to gauge the effect. Sponge is more absorbent than rubber, so you will need to use more paint.

USING MINIATURE INKPADS

These small inkpads come in a range of brilliant colours and metallics. Just wipe them across the rubber stamp. As with brush application you can use more than one colour at a time, but take care to avoid colours mixing on the stamp pads.

USING A GLAZE

You can apply a translucent colour glaze using a stamp or potato cut. Make up some wallpaper paste and tint it with liquid watercolour paint or water-based ink. Dip the stamp in and print. The paste dries to a clear sheen with a hint of colour.

PAINT EFFECTS

CREATING DIFFERENT EFFECTS

The same rubber stamp can be made to have several different characteristics, depending on the colours and inks that you choose. The sun stamp below illustrates this very well and has been used to create cool and warm effects.

1 This metallic print was made with equal parts PVA glue and water, to half of metallic powder. This mixture was applied to the stamp with a rubber roller. When dry, the glittering powder is held in a transparent glaze.

2 The same sun stamp was coated with two different coloured paints, applied with a brush. When paint is applied in this way, it is possible to separate areas of colour, which is impossible when using an inkpad.

LIGHT EFFECTS

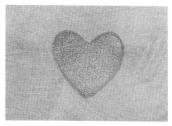

This effect combines the softness of a pink colourwashed wall with the almost powdery appearance of a medium-density sponge stamp lightly applied to the wall. Emulsion paint was mixed half and half with prepared wallpaper paste, which gives a gelatinous quality when wet and a transparent glaze once dry.

OVERPRINTING EFFECTS

Once you have cut a complicated design like the one below, you can experiment with building up the pattern by adding colour and overprinting. This design is unusual because it can be printed one way, then turned around to print in the other direction. The second print made on top of the first actually fills in the triangle shapes that were originally left blank. This works particularly well for the central pattern. Care must be taken not to re-ink the border lines, because they are less effective when printed with more than one colour.

1 The first print was made in light yellow emulsion on to a light blue colourwashed wall.

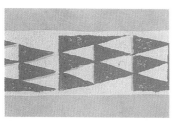

2 The stamp was cleaned and re-inked with a dark blue-grey paint, avoiding the thin border edging. The print was made with the stamp turned around to face the other direction, but lined up to fit exactly on top of the first print.

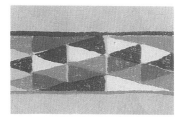

3 Other colours were applied to selected areas of the stamp including a separate colour for each of the border lines.

SPECIAL-EFFECT PAINT MIXTURES

There are many different kinds of paint available these days and they are often sold in huge self-service warehouses. Sometimes it is impossible to find any specialist assistance for your particular project. In this book we have tried to narrow down the paint options by suggesting either acrylic artist's colour, watercolour (available as a ready-mixed liquid) or emulsion paint. This should not mean that all paint finishes look the same; there are a number of very simple ways to vary the intensity and texture of these paints, using wallpaper paste and PVA glue. The step-by-step photographs below explain the different methods and effects that can be achieved.

WATERCOLOUR PAINT AND WALLPAPER PASTE

This mixture is only suitable for surfaces that do not need wiping clean, so use it for paper and card but not for walls.

1 Mix the wallpaper paste to a slightly thinner consistency than usual. It will thicken after five minutes, when you will be able to thin it by adding more water. It should have a sloppy consistency.

2 Add a drop of ready-mixed watercolour paint, sold in small jars by art and craft suppliers. The colour is intense and a small amount goes a long way. Add and stir in as many drops as you need, testing the paint on a sheet of scrap paper to judge the brightness. The paste gives the thickness that is needed for stamping – watercolour paint on its own would not be suitable.

EMULSION PAINT AND WALLPAPER PASTE

This mixture adds another dimension to the usual texture of emulsion paint; and the wallpaper paste
makes it particularly suited to sponge stamping.

1 Mix up a glaze using one part
emulsion paint to two parts wallpaper
paste. Mix the wallpaper paste with
the required amount of water first,
then stir in the emulsion. The
advantage of this mixture is that it is
washable when dry, so it is suitable for
all household decorating work. The
wallpaper paste dries transparent and
adds a glazed texture to the emulsion.
Its gelatinous quality works well with
sponge stamps.

2 When you have achieved the
desired colour and consistency, prop
up one side of the plate with a small
wooden block, or something similar –
the plate should feel stable and remain
in this position to provide an even
coating of paint for stamping.

3 Soak the foam stamp in a bowl of
water. All foam works a lot better for
stamping if it is damp rather than dry
as it will absorb and release the paint
mixture more readily.

4 Lift the stamp out of the water and
squeeze out the excess moisture into a
sheet of absorbent kitchen paper.

5 Scoop up some of the paint and use
it to coat the raised side of the plate
with a thin layer of colour. Dip the
foam stamp into this.

6 Make a test print on to a sheet of
scrap paper to ensure that the stamp is
not overloaded with paint. This is the
final fish stamp printed on a light blue
colourwashed background.

DESIGNING WITH STAMPS

Once you have realized the potential of the instant print, you may want to explore more creative ways of using stamps. Variety can be achieved by changing colours in a sequence or inverting, rotating or grouping stamped images. Just think of all the basic pattern formations – stripes, zig-zags, diagonals, crosses, waves and many more. All of these design techniques can be used to add style and interest to your stamped patterns.

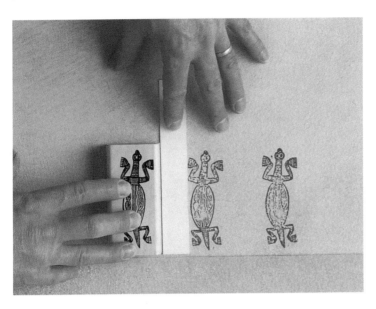

REGIMENTED ROWS

When creating a basic row of stamped prints, good spacing is vital. Decide on the space between the stamped prints and cut a paper strip to that width. Position the stamp in the corner of the paper or wall to be stamped and make the first print. Align the paper strip against the stamp block and, holding it steady, lift up the stamp and position it on the other side of the paper strip to make the next print. Continue in this way to complete the row of stamps. Use a paper strip to measure the distance between the rows, checking the 90-degree angle with a set square.

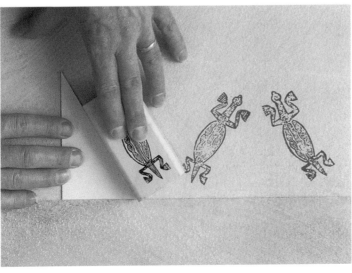

ZIGZAG LIZARDS

To make a zigzag pattern, cut out a triangle with one 90-degree angle and the longest side at least as long as the stamp block. Fit the 90-degree angle into the corner of the paper with the stamp lined up against the slanted edge. Print the first image, then flip the triangle over, line it up with the bottom edge of the paper, and make the second print slanting away from the first. Flip it again without altering the position of the vertical side, and stamp the third print on the slant. Continue this way along the row.

CUT-OUT PRINTS

Sometimes the spacing of a design is difficult to visualize. Using paper cut-out prints will help enormously. This method is particularly useful when planning a design for fabric or walls. Make enough stamped prints to give a clear idea of how the repeat motifs will work, and cut out the shapes. Arrange them in rows on your chosen background, to help you make decisions on spacing.

EXPERIMENTING ON PAPER

The paper cut-out prints are also useful when designing different styles of pattern. Use them to decide whether to overlap the stamps or leave spaces between them. Sometimes the eye is the best judge of what is comfortable spacially, regardless of regular measured distances. Stand back from your designs and half-close your eyes to determine the most pleasing proportion of positive and negative shapes.

CREATIVE DESIGNS

Creative arrangements can be fine-tuned with paper cut-out shapes before you commit to them permanently.

Rubber stamps are usually quite small. If you would like to use a particular rubber stamp but need a larger motif then consider using the stamp repeated in a formation to turn it into a much larger pattern.

Experiment with the prints in box shapes, spirals, circles and triangles; each one will look quite different from the rest.

Walls & Surfaces

DECORATING should not be a high-anxiety activity; it should be enjoyable to do and rewarding to view. Stamping is not only both of these, but also the quickest and easiest way to put a pattern on a wall.

There are many different looks that you can achieve with stamps, depending upon the materials you use. A pre-cut rubber stamp like the one used for the wallpaper project produces a fine, sophisticated and subtle effect when used in blue on a cream background. Change to a silver ink on deep blue and it will take on a mystical personality, and sunshine-yellow on sky-blue will create a happy, summery look.

Home-made foam stamps will create a completely different look. They can be quite detailed when cut from high-density foam, like the Scandinavian motifs, or simple and bold like the medium-density sponge Sunstar. The prints will vary depending on the amount and consistency of the paint you use. A transparent colour, for instance, can be made by adding wallpaper paste to emulsion paint, and a dazzling gold can be made by mixing bronze powder with PVA glue. There are some great new "chalky" paints on the market that mimic the effect of the old distempers, and they leave a slightly raised print on the walls.

It is not only the type of foam or paint that you use that affects the print, but also the way you use your stamp. If you always use the same amount of pressure and paint, then you will have a regular pattern of identical motifs. If you want a more handpainted look, then make more prints before you re-charge your stamp and vary the pressure you use - the resulting prints will have an irregular and slightly faded look.

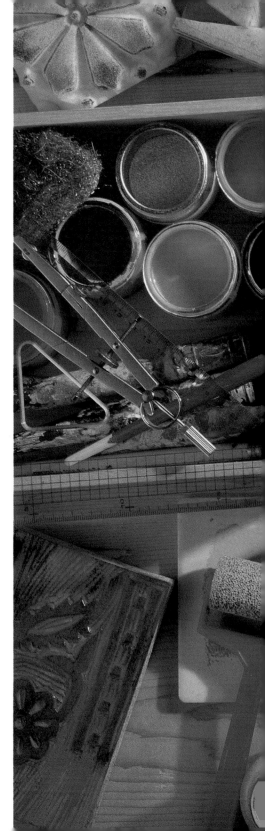

SURFACE APPLICATION

When you print with stamps, the shape remains constant but there are many different possible finishes that can be achieved. The factors affecting these are the surface that you stamp on to, the material used to make up the stamp, and the substance that you stamp with. These can vary enormously, and to illustrate some of the possible effects we have printed two motifs with emulsion paint and experimented with different finishes.

ALTERING EFFECTS

Once the pattern has been stamped on the wall, there are different ways that you can alter its regular appearance.

1 This is the basic version of the design. A foam stamp was pressed into blue emulsion and used to make an even print on an emulsion-painted wall.

2 The print was allowed to dry and then it was lightly rubbed back using fine-grade sandpaper.

3 This stamp was printed in the same way as the first one, but then darkened with a coat of tinted antiquing varnish. As well as protecting the surface, it deepens the original colour and adds a slight sheen.

DEPTH EFFECTS

Varnish can be used over your stamped designs to add depth to the colour and protect the wall surface. These three prints, made with a polystyrene stamp, demonstrate the changes that coats of varnish can make.

1 This is the basic stamped pattern in grey emulsion on a light buttermilk-coloured background.

2 This is the same surface after one coat of tinted varnish was applied. This has deepened the yellow tone considerably.

3 A second coat of the same varnish was applied and the colour has turned deep pine-yellow. Tinted varnish comes in many shades, and it enriches the colour with each application.

HANDPRINTED SUN WALLPAPER

Handprinted wallpaper is a genuine luxury and as such costs a small fortune. This project shows you how to make your own wallpaper for a fraction of the cost.

Unlike most rubber stamping projects, this one needs a certain amount of pre-planning and a long, clear work surface, such as a wallpaper-pasting table. The paint used is emulsion, which is fast-drying, but care must still be taken not to smudge the pattern as you move along the paper.

Measure the walls to be covered, adding approximately 2 metres/2 yards to allow for pattern matching. Lining paper was used here, which comes in a natural off-white colour. It is the least expensive wallpaper available but there are finer-quality plain papers on the market that you may prefer to use.

YOU WILL NEED

- *ruler*
- *felt-tipped pen*
- *sun motif rubber stamp*
- *paper strip the width of the wallpaper*
- *pencil*
- *small roller tray or plate*
- *emulsion paint in turquoise-green*
- *small rubber roller*
- *wallpaper paste*
- *pasting brush*

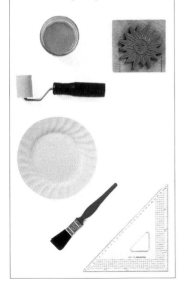

1 Use a ruler to draw lines that butt up against the extremities of the sun stamp. Extend these around the sides of the stamp, so that the exact position of the shape is visibly marked.

2 Make a measuring guide with a strip of paper. Mark out the width of six stamps along the paper strip.

3 Place the the measuring guide along the bottom edge of the wallpaper. Charge the stamp with paint using the roller. Make a test print to ensure that the stamp is not overloaded.

4 Make the first stamp print in the second section; the next in the fourth and the last in the sixth, lining them up along the measuring strip.

5 Place the paper measuring guide along the side edge of the wallpaper, making light pencil marks as a guide.

6 Reposition the measuring strip horizontally and print the next row of motifs in the first, third and fifth sections. Move the stamp up using the vertical pencil marks as a guide and print the third row in the same positions as the first. Continue in this way until the wallpaper is completed.

7 Hang the wallpaper to form a continuous pattern, matching up the rows of suns with a final row resting on the dado rail.

SCANDINAVIAN LIVING-ROOM

Create a cool atmosphere with this sophisticated Gustavian-influenced wall stamping.
This project is less instant than others featured in the book, but the elegance of the result justifies all the
preparatory work. The stamps are cut from high-density foam which is mounted on to blocks of hardboard,
and a small door knob is added for easy handling. Before any stamping can be done, a grid must be drawn
across the wall using a plumb line and a cardboard square.
If you find the effect of the two blues too cool, you can add warmth by applying a coat of tinted varnish to the
whole wall, including the woodwork. It has the effect of bathing the room in golden sunlight.

YOU WILL NEED

- ◆ wood glue or PVA glue
- ◆ 2 pieces hardboard,
  9cm x 9cm / 3½in x 3½in
- ◆ 2 pieces high-density foam,
  such as upholstery foam,
  9cm x 9cm / 3½in x 3½in
- ◆ tracing paper
- ◆ pencil
- ◆ spray adhesive
- ◆ scalpel
- ◆ ruler
- ◆ 2 small wooden door knobs
- ◆ plumb line
- ◆ card, 18cm x 18cm / 7in x 7in
- ◆ plate
- ◆ emulsion paint in dark blue
- ◆ square-tipped paintbrush

1 Apply wood glue to the hardboard squares and stick the foam on to them. Leave the glue to dry.

2 Trace and transfer the pattern shapes from the template section. Lightly spray with adhesive and place on the foam blocks.

3 Cut around the edges of the designs and remove the paper pattern. Scoop out the background to leave the stamp standing proud of the hardboard.

4 Draw two intersecting lines across the back of the hardboard and glue a wooden door knob in the centre.

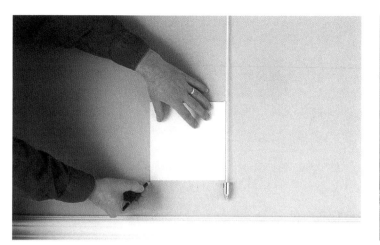

5 Attach a plumb line at ceiling height to give a vertical guideline (this can be done with a piece of Blu-tack). Mark a point 8cm/3¼in above the dado rail and place one corner of the card square on it, lined up along the plumb line. Mark all the corners on the wall in pencil, then move the square up, continuing to mark the corners. Use this system to mark a grid of squares across the whole upper wall.

6 One of the stamps has a static motif and the other has a swirl. Use the static one first, dipping it into a plate coated with paint and making the first print on a sheet of scrap paper to ensure that the stamp is not overloaded. Then print up the wall, from the 8cm/3¼in mask.

7 Continue printing, working up the diagonal.

8 Change to the swirl motif, and stamp this pattern in the spaces between the static motifs.

9 Use a pencil and ruler to draw a
line 3.5cm/1½in above the dado rail.

10 Fill the space between the pencil
line and the dado rail with dark blue
paint using a square-tipped paintbrush.

SUNSTAR WALL

It is hard to believe that decorating can be this easy. Gone are the days of the perfectly even finish of flat colour - now we are more attuned to the comfort of patchy paintwork. If you have a minute and a piece of sponge to spare, that is all it takes to make the sunstar stamp. It could not be simpler.
The wall was colourwashed with diluted coffee-coloured emulsion paint. Just mix the paint half and half with water, stir well and paint the wall using random sweeping strokes. Work within an arm's reach and blend any hard edges with a dryish brush before the paint dries.

YOU WILL NEED

- medium-density sponge, such as a kitchen sponge
- felt-tipped pen
- scalpel
- plumb line
- card, 25cm x 25cm / 10in x 10in
- pencil
- wallpaper paste, for mixing
- cup
- plate
- emulsion paint in terracotta
- paintbrush

1 Draw a circle on the sponge using a round object as a template.

2 Draw the shape of the sunstar within the circle, referring to the pattern in the template section. The shape can be made to any size.

3 Cut out the circle with a scalpel. Cut around the shape first, then cut all the way through.

4 Cut around the drawn pattern shape and discard the sponge offcuts.

5 Attach a plumb line at ceiling height (this can be done with a lump of Blu-tack). Place the card square on the diagonal behind the line, so that it falls through two points. Mark all the corners on the wall in pencil, then move the square up, continuing to mark all the corners. Use this system, moving the line along the wall, until a grid of pencil marks covers the wall.

6 Mix a cup of wallpaper paste, place a dollop on the plate alongside an equal amount of terracotta paint and blend the two together with a paintbrush. Press the sponge into the mixture and make a test print on a sheet of scrap paper. Then start stamping the wall, using the pencil marks as your guide. Mix the paste and paint together as you go, so that the density of the colour varies.

7 Continue stamping so that the sunstars form a regular pattern across the whole wall.

MEXICAN HALLWAY

Banish gloomy weather with vibrant sunshine-yellow and intense sky-blue in the hallway. With the heat turned up, it will be time to add an ethnic touch by stamping an Aztec border along the walls.
Use the patterns from the template section to cut basic geometric shapes from a medium-density sponge, like the ones used for washing dishes. Mix shades of green with purples, add an earthy red and then stamp on diamonds of fuschia-pink for its sheer brilliance. It's a bold statement.
These days emulsion paint is available in a huge range of exciting colours. Try not to be tempted by muted colours for this border - it will lose much of its impact. Bright colours go well with natural materials, like straw hats, sisal matting, wicker baskets and clay pots.

YOU WILL NEED

- ◆ *tape measure*
- ◆ *spirit level*
- ◆ *pencil*
- ◆ *emulsion paint in sunshine-yellow and deep sky-blue*
- ◆ *paint rollers and tray*
- ◆ *small amounts emulsion paint in light blue-grey, purple, brick-red, fuschia-pink and dark green*
- ◆ *5 plates*
- ◆ *foam strip*
- ◆ *medium-density sponge, such as a kitchen sponge, cut into the pattern shapes from the template section*

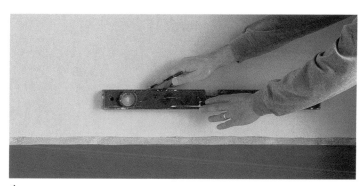

1 Divide the wall at dado rail height using a tape measure, spirit level and pencil. Paint the upper part sunshine-yellow and the lower part deep sky-blue, using the paint roller. Then use the spirit level and pencil to draw a parallel line approximately 15cm/6in above the blue section.

2 Use a foam strip to stamp a light blue-grey line directly above the blue section. Then use the strip to stamp the top line of the border along the pencil line.

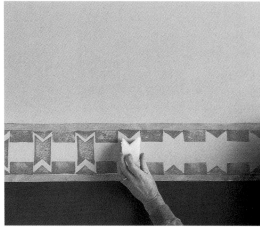

3 Spread an even coating of each of the frieze colours on to separate plates. Use the rectangular and triangular shapes alternately to print a purple row above the bottom line and below the top line. Stamp on to scrap paper first to make sure the stamp is not overloaded.

4 Stamp the largest shape in brick-red, lining it up to fit between the points of the top and bottom triangles. There should be approximately 1cm/⅓in of background colour showing between this brick-red shape and the purple triangles.

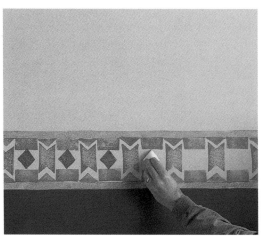

5 Stamp the diamond shapes in fuschia-pink between the central brick-red motifs.

6 Finally add a zigzagged edge by overprinting dark green triangles along the light blue-grey lines.

SPINNING SUN MOTIF

This rich combination of spicy red-brown and earthy yellow seems to infuse the room with warmth and the spinning sun motif has a timeless quality. The pattern is great fun to paint, because once you've marked out the grid, it grows very quickly, and using a single colour makes for very easy stamping.
Colourwash the wall with yellow-ochre emulsion paint, diluted half and half with water. Use random brushstrokes, working within arm's reach. The finish should look patchy rather than even - like dappled sunlight. Paint the lower section a deep terracotta.

YOU WILL NEED

- ◆ tape measure
- ◆ spirit level
- ◆ pencil
- ◆ paintbrush
- ◆ emulsion paint in terracotta and yellow-ochre
- ◆ clear satin varnish
- ◆ tracing paper
- ◆ scalpel
- ◆ adhesive spray
- ◆ high-density foam, such as upholstery foam
- ◆ plate
- ◆ plumb line
- ◆ card 15cm x 15cm/6in x 5in

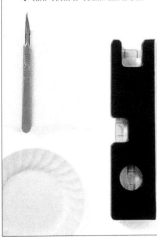

1 Divide the wall at dado rail height, using a tape measure, spirit level and pencil. Paint terracotta below the line and yellow-ochre above. Apply a coat of clear satin varnish to the terracotta. Trace, transfer and cut out the pattern shapes from the template section. Lightly spray with adhesive and place them on the foam. Cut around the designs with a scalpel.

2 Spread an even coating of terracotta paint on to a plate and press the smaller stamp into it. Make a test print on scrap paper to ensure that the stamp is not overloaded with paint, then stamp a row above the dado line. Attach a plumb line at ceiling height, and mark out a grid using the card and a pencil, as described earlier in the Sunstar Wall project.

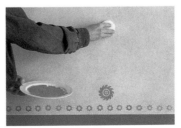

3 Press the larger stamp into the terracotta paint and test print on scrap paper. Using the pencil marks as the baseline, stamp the large sunwheels on the wall.

4 Connect the sunwheels by stamping three small sunstars in a straight line between them, across the whole surface of the wall.

FLORAL SPRIG

*This all-over country floral motif is made with three sponge stamps. The background colour is creamy yellow
and the sprigs echo the colours used on and below the dado rail.
The sprigs change direction with every alternate print, giving the pattern its dynamic energy. Vary the intensity of the colour
by applying less pressure on some prints, as well as making several prints before re-charging your sponge.
The most time-consuming part of the project will be marking out a grid of pencil marks across the whole wall surface,
but once that is in place the stamped pattern will grow very quickly. This pattern
will suit a large or small room equally well.*

YOU WILL NEED
- *tracing paper*
- *pencil*
- *spray adhesive*
- *low-density sponge, such as a bath sponge*
- *felt-tipped pen*
- *scalpel*
- *paper, 14cm x 14cm / 5½in x 5½in*
- *plumb line*
- *2 plates*
- *emulsion paint in brick-red and dusky blue*

1 Trace, transfer and cut out the pattern shapes from the template section. Lightly spray the shapes with adhesive and place on the sponge. Use a scalpel to cut out the shapes.

2 Attach a plumb line at ceiling height to drop down to dado rail height. Place the card square on the diagonal, with the plumb line running through the centre. Mark all the corners on the wall in pencil. Move the square up and continue to use this system to mark a grid on the wall.

3 Spread the red and blue paint on to separate plates. Make the first print on to scrap paper to make sure that the stamp is not overloaded. Using the pencil marks as your guide, stamp blue stem shapes. Change the direction of the curve from left to right with each alternate print.

4 Use the same blue paint to stamp the leaf shape on to the base of each stem, alternating the direction of each print as you did with the stem.

5 Dip the flower-shaped sponge into the brick-red paint. Make an initial print on scrap paper to ensure the stamp is not overloaded. Stamp the flower shapes on to the tops of the stems. Vary the pressure used, to give different densities of colour.

CORK-STAMPED FLOORBOARDS

This aesthetically pleasing stamp has been made from seven wine bottle corks. They have been taped together in a daisy-shaped bundle and the pattern shapes are cut from the surface of the cork bundle with a scalpel. Dense cork like this is a wonderful material to carve into, being both soft and very smooth. Use the stamp on sanded wood or cork tiles with a dark woodstain, allowing it to stand and soak up the stain for ten minutes before you begin printing. We have used it as a border but it could also be spaced across the floor as an all-over pattern.

YOU WILL NEED

- *7 wine bottle corks*
- *wood glue or PVA glue*
- *strong adhesive tape*
- *felt-tipped pen*
- *scalpel*
- *2 paper strips of equal width*
- *dark woodstain*
- *bowl*
- *kitchen paper*

1 Stand the seven corks in a daisy formation on a sheet of paper. Apply a line of wood glue to all their meeting edges. Make sure that all their ends are flat on the paper before the glue hardens. This will provide a level printing surface and a better result.

2 When the glue has become tacky, surround the bundle with a tight binding of strong adhesive tape.

3 Copy the pattern shape from the template section with a felt-tipped pen on to the flat surface of the corks.

4 Cut away all the background pieces with a scalpel.

➤

41

5 The pattern can be made more complex by cutting grooves in the smooth cork surface.

6 Before printing, ensure the floor surface is totally dust-free. Use the two paper strips as spacing guides: lay them against the skirting board in both directions from a corner. Allow the stamp to stand in a bowl of woodstain for ten minutes, then blot it on kitchen paper. Make the first stamp in the corner.

7 Move the spacing strips into the next corner and stamp the second print there.

8 Move the strips along the straight skirting board section and stamp a motif about halfway between the first two. Stamp a row of evenly spaced motifs between the existing prints. Continue to stamp a border around the room.

LEOPARD-SKIN SKIRTING`BOARD

Leopard-skin patterns never go out of fashion and they always make a very bold statement. If you are hesitant about trying this design, why not test it out in a small room, such as a cloakroom. The advantage of this is that you won't have to change the furniture to match the style.

Team the leopard-skin skirting boards with stunning hot-pink walls if you dare, or deep green for more of a jungle feel. This pattern works well in a very theatrical setting with plenty of lush velvet and gilding, or could be combined with a stark high-tech style.

YOU WILL NEED

- ♦ low-density sponge, such as a bath sponge
- ♦ felt-tipped pen
- ♦ scalpel
- ♦ emulsion paint in sunshine-yellow and dark brown
- ♦ paintbrushes
- ♦ plate
- ♦ clear matt varnish

1 Copy the pattern shapes from the template section on to the surface of the sponge with a felt-tipped pen.

2 Cut out the individual shapes with a scalpel. First cut around the shape then part the sponge and cut right through.

3 Paint the skirting board in sunshine-yellow and allow to dry.

4 Spread an even coating of dark brown paint on a plate and dip one of the shapes into it. Stamp on to a sheet of scrap paper first, to ensure that the sponge stamp is not overloaded, then begin stamping the skirting board.

5 Use the individual shapes to build up the leopard-skin pattern. Hold a sheet of scrap paper against the edge of the skirting to protect the floor, then overprint, so that only partial shapes appear in some places. This makes an all-over pattern look more convincing.

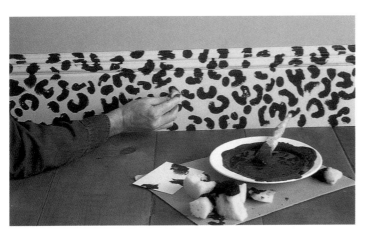

6 Stand back and look for any obvious gaps in the pattern, then use the small shapes to fill them in. Allow the leopard-skin pattern to dry.

7 Finish the skirting with a coat of varnish. Here, clear matt varnish was used, but you could use a tinted or satin varnish for a different effect.

GREEK KEY BATHROOM

This bathroom looks far too smart to have been decorated by an amateur. The border design is a classic Greek key interspaced with a bold square and cross. The black and gold look stunning on a pure white tiled wall. Every bathroom has different features, so use the border to make the most of the best ones, while drawing attention away from the duller areas. If you like a co-ordinated scheme, you could print a border on a set of towels, using fabric inks.

YOU WILL NEED
- ♦ *tracing paper*
- ♦ *pencil*
- ♦ *spray adhesive*
- ♦ *high-density foam, such as upholstery foam*
- ♦ *scalpel*
- ♦ *acrylic enamel paint in black and gold*
- ♦ *2 plates*
- ♦ *wooden baton 2-3cm/¾-1¼in wide, depending on the bathroom*
- ♦ *masking tape*

1 Trace and transfer the pattern shapes from the template section. Lightly spray the shapes with adhesive and place them on the foam. To cut out the shapes, cut the outline first, then undercut and remove any excess, leaving the pattern shape standing proud of the foam.

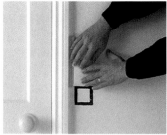

2 Apply an even coating of black paint on to a plate. Place the baton up next to the door frame to keep the border an even distance from it. Make a test print on scrap paper then begin by stamping one black outline square in the bottom corner, at dado rail height. Print a key shape above it, being careful not to smudge the adjoining edge of the previous print.

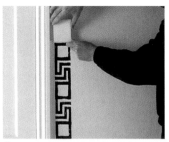

3 Continue alternating the stamps around the door frame.

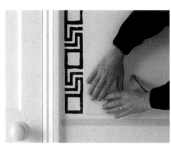

4 Mark the base line at dado rail height with masking tape and alternate the designs along this line.

5 Place a coating of gold paint on to a plate and dip the cross shape into it. Make a test print on scrap paper, then print the shape in the square frames.

SEASCAPE BATHROOM FRIEZE

*This really is instant decorating. The sponge shapes come from a child's sea-life painting set. Other themed
sets available include jungle, dinosaur, transport and farm animals.
Although these are children's sponges, the project is not intended for an exclusively child-oriented bathroom
scheme. The shapes are appropriate for grown-ups, too. They can also be used to decorate
other rooms in the home.*

YOU WILL NEED
- *ruler*
- *pencil*
- *spirit level*
- *emulsion paint in cream, brick-red and blue*
- *3 plates*
- *seaside-themed children's painting sponges*

1 Draw a line for the base of your frieze, using a ruler, pencil and spirit level.
Spread the paints on to separate plates and press the shapes into the paint following
a sequence of cream, brick-red and blue. Make test prints on scrap paper to ensure
that the sponges are not overloaded. Print all the sponge shapes across the base
line, then repeat the sequence to make another row.

2 Partially overprint each shape by dipping each sponge into a different colour
from the one first used.

3 Continue overprinting the shapes. The second colour adds a shadow effect, giving the shapes a more three-dimensional appearance.

CHECKS AND CHERRIES WINDOW

Bring the flavour of the French countryside into your kitchen with checks and cherries. These popular designs
are found adorning all kinds of crockery, enamelware, fabrics, pelmets and furniture in rural France.
The checked border is applied with an ingenious self-inking rubber roller stamp, which is so easy to use you
could get carried away. Be careful, though, because too many of these checks could become overpowering.
Stamp the cherries randomly to make an all-over pattern. Leave plenty of space between the prints in order to
prevent the pattern from looking too busy. Keep the whole effect light and airy.

YOU WILL NEED
♦ *masking tape*
♦ *square-tipped 2.5cm/1in paintbrush*
♦ *emulsion paint in maize-yellow*
♦ *scrap paper*
♦ *check-pattern rubber roller stamp*
♦ *cherry motif rubber stamp*
♦ *red inkpad*

1 Mark the border around the window frame, either applying masking tape along the outer edge or marking it with light pencil guidelines. Paint the border maize–yellow.

2 Mitre the corners for the roller stamp by positioning a sheet of scrap paper at a 45-degree angle, continuing the line of the mitred window frame. Hold the paper in place with tape.

3 Run the roller stamp down, following the edge of the yellow border and overprinting the mitring paper. Do this in one movement.

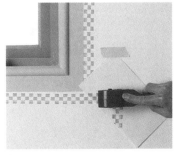

4 Flip the paper over, keeping the same angle, and run the roller stamp across the bottom of the border. Overprint the paper then remove it.

5 Use the red stamp inkpad and the cherry stamp to make a well-spaced pattern all over the surrounding wall.

FURNITURE & FURNISHINGS

MAKE IT A RULE never to pass by a junk shop without glancing in. It's not that stamping is unsuitable for new furniture, just that doing up old junk is so rewarding. And you are far less likely to be experimental with a brand new chair than with one that actually needs some life breathing into it!

Of course, there are always exceptions. White melamine kitchen units, for example can be given a new identity with matt oil-based paint and a selection of stamps.

You can use emulsion paint to stamp patterns on to bare or painted wood, and the designs can be protected by a coat of varnish. If the wood has been previously painted with varnish or an oil-based gloss, just rub away the shine with sandpaper to give the paint a matt texture to key into.

The star cupboard project makes use of other techniques as well: paint has been stamped with stars that have been overpainted, rubbed back, sandpapered and varnished. The end result is a layered look that really glows. The contemporary shelf was so insignificant before, but its potato-cut edging has changed it into a stylish focal point. And who would have thought that an occasional table could be rubber stamped and given a completely new image?

As with all the projects in the book, all you need to do is get started, then you will realize the tremendous potential of stamping. There are very few surfaces that can't be decorated in this way. Whichever project you choose to start with, don't worry about making mistakes; after all, stamping only takes a little while to do, so it can be re-done just as quickly!

WOOD APPLICATION

You can use most types of paint on wood, although some will need sealing with a protective coat of varnish. New wood needs to be sealed with a coat of shellac on knotting - this stops resin leaking through the grain.

Below are some examples of rubber, sponge and potato prints made on wood with a variety of media. Woodstains, varnishes and paints have different properties and create different effects depending on the stamp used.

This print was made with emulsion paint applied with a potato cut.

This print was made with emulsion paint applied with a sponge stamp.

This print was made with emulsion paint applied with a rubber stamp.

This print was made with wood dye applied with a sponge stamp.

This print was made with wood dye applied with a rubber stamp.

This print was made with wood dye applied with a potato cut.

This print was made with tinted varnish applied with a rubber stamp.

This print was made with tinted varnish applied with a potato cut.

This print was made with red ink applied with a potato cut.

COUNTRY-STYLE SHELF

Simple in shape but conveying a universally understood message, the heart has been used in folk art for centuries. Here, the outline of a heart was drawn in four positions on a high-density foam block, then cut out to make a stamp that resembles a four-leafed clover. The smaller heart is a traditional solid shape that fits neatly along the edges of the shelf supports.

The background colour was applied in three separate coats: the first one was painted directly on to the bare wood, then rubbed back slightly with a damp cloth; a second colour was applied and rubbed back in the same way; then a final lighter colour went over the top. When the shelf was dry, it was sanded with medium-grade sandpaper, to reveal some of the grain and layers of colour.

YOU WILL NEED

- ◆ *tracing paper*
- ◆ *pencil*
- ◆ *spray adhesive*
- ◆ *high-density foam, such as upholstery foam*
- ◆ *scalpel*
- ◆ *acrylic or emulsion paint in deep red*
- ◆ *plate*
- ◆ *paintbrush*
- ◆ *country-style shelf, painted as described above*

1 Trace and transfer the pattern shapes from the template section. Lightly spray the shapes with adhesive and place them on the foam. Cut around the outline of the shapes with a scalpel.

2 Cut out the single heart shape. First cut the outline, then part the foam and cut all the way through.

3 Use the stamp as a measuring guide to estimate the number of prints that will fit comfortably along the back of the shelf. Mark their positions lightly in pencil. Spread an even coating of deep red paint on a plate.

4 Make a test print of the clover-leaf stamp on scrap paper to ensure that the stamp is not overloaded with paint. (You may find it easier to apply paint to the stamp with a paintbrush.) Referring to the pencil guidelines, press the stamp into the paint and make the first print on the wood.

5 Continue until you have completed all of the clover-leaf shapes. Try not to get the finish too even; this is a rustic piece of furniture and an uneven finish will be more suitable.

6 Finish off the shelf with a row of small hearts along the support edges, then add one between each of the larger motifs.

FOLK MOTIF CHAIR

Old kitchen chairs are functional and comfortable but often very plain.
This particular chair was just begging for a make-over and is now the centre of attention.
This modular style of decoration allows you to unite a non-matching set of chairs by stamping them with
similar designs in the same colours. They will look much more interesting than a new set,
and will have cost a fraction of the price.
All you need to do is cut out the five pattern elements using a scalpel and you are ready to go.

YOU WILL NEED
♦ *emulsion paint in light blue-grey*
♦ *paintbrushes*
♦ *ruler*
♦ *pencil*
♦ *acrylic or emulsion paint in red, white*
and dark blue-grey
♦ *plate*
♦ *medium-density sponge, such as a*
kitchen sponge, cut into the pattern shapes
from the template section
♦ *clear matt varnish*

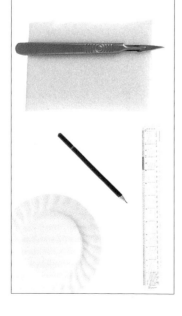

1 Give the chair at least two coats of light blue-grey emulsion paint and leave to dry. To achieve a "weathered" look, you could rub back the paint between coats, to let some of the grain show through. Use a ruler to find the centre of the back rest and make a small pencil mark.

2 Use a plate as your palette and spread out an even coating of red, white and dark blue-grey acrylic or emulsion paint. Press the diamond shape into the red paint and make a test print to ensure the stamp is not overloaded with paint. Stamp the diamond shape.

3 Stamp a white circle on either side of the diamond.

4 Stamp a dark blue-grey triangle and finally a red half-moon shape on either side, to form a symmetrical pattern.

5 Using the small square shape, stamp dark blue-grey diamonds around the edge of the back rest with equally sized gaps in between.

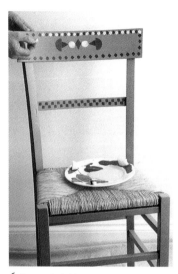

6 Stamp dark blue-grey squares on the back crossbar, as shown. Then fill in the gaps on the back rest with white diamonds and the gaps on the back crossbar with white squares.

7 Stamp dark blue-grey triangles, pointing outwards, to form a "sawtooth" border, down the sides of the chair back.

8 Stamp red circles on the front legs where the lower crossbars meet them. Stamp dark blue-grey triangles above and below the circles, pointing outwards. Add some dark blue-grey and white diamonds to the centres of the lower crossbars. Finally, when all the paint is dry, give the whole chair a coat of clear matt varnish to protect the design.

STAR CUPBOARD

This attractive little cupboard seems to fit in the moment you have finished it. While its style is individual, it does not scream out for attention, and it has that comfortable, lived-in look.
The cupboard was painted, stamped, then painted again. Finally, it was given a coat of antiquing varnish and rubbed back with a cloth in places. It glows from all the attention and took just one afternoon to make. This style of decoration is so simple that you might consider transforming other items of furniture in the same way.

YOU WILL NEED
♦ *wooden wall cupboard*
♦ *emulsion paint in olive-green, off-white and vermilion*
♦ *paintbrushes*
♦ *2 plates*
♦ *medium-density sponge, such as a kitchen sponge, cut into the pattern shape from the template section*
♦ *PVA glue*
♦ *matt varnish in antique pine*
♦ *kitchen cloth*

1 Paint the cupboard with a coat of olive-green emulsion, applying a second coat if necessary.

2 Spread some off-white emulsion paint on to a plate. Dip the sponge star shape into the paint and print the stars all over the cupboard, quite close together.

3 Make a mixture of two-thirds vermilion paint and one-third PVA glue. When the stars have dried, coat the cupboard with a liberal amount of this colour, daubed on with a brush.

4 Finish the cupboard with a coat of tinted varnish, then use a cloth to rub some of it off each of the stars. This layering of colour gives the surface its rich patina.

NONSENSE KEY CUPBOARD

If you have a well-developed sense of the ridiculous, then this project will appeal to you. The idea is to use three totally unconnected images of varying scales to form a nonsense design. Our choice was three Morris dancers below a large, old-fashioned tap, surrounded by stars, but you could choose anything you wished. The wooden cupboard was painted with white primer before the stamps were added in dark blue ink. The colour was applied with a fine artist's paintbrush using bright watercolour paint. The streaky paint finish was achieved with yellow watercolour wiped on with a small piece of sponge.

YOU WILL NEED

- ◆ *small key cupboard*
- ◆ *white wood primer*
- ◆ *paintbrush*
- ◆ *selection of stamps*
- ◆ *navy-blue permanent inkpad*
- ◆ *scrap paper*
- ◆ *scalpel*
- ◆ *fine artist's paintbrush*
- ◆ *watercolour paints*
- ◆ *clear matt varnish (optional)*
- ◆ *medium-grade sandpaper*

1 Apply two coats of white wood primer to the bare wood of the key cupboard, allowing the primer to dry thoroughly between coats.

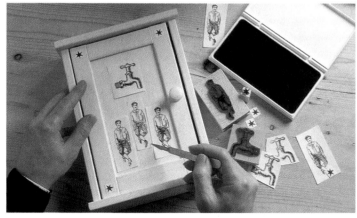

2 Stamp the motifs on to scrap paper. Cut them out and use them to plan your design by positioning the paper pieces on to the cupboard.

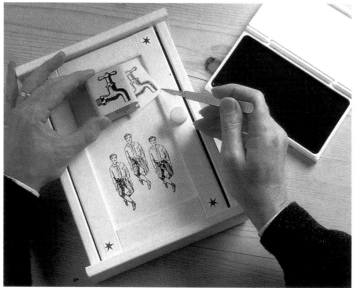

3 When you are happy with your layout, stamp the designs directly on to the cupboard. Use the paper scraps as a guide by moving them out of the way at the last moment.

4 Stamp a small star in each corner of the cupboard.

5 Begin to paint the details using watercolour paints and a fine paintbrush. Fill in the first colour.

6 Continue filling in the details of the other stamps, adding more colour.

7 Complete the details and allow to dry. When the paint has dried, use a small piece of sponge to wipe yellow watercolour paint over the cupboard avoiding the central, illustrated panel.

▼ *For a quicker finish, leave the details and background unpainted. The combination of blue and white creates a more cooling effect than vibrant primaries.*

8 When the paint has dried, lightly rub back the yellow with sandpaper. If desired, seal the surface with a coat of clear varnish.

CONTEMPORARY SHELF

Although nursery methods have been employed to decorate this shelf, the result is an incredibly sophisticated
room feature. The shelf pattern has been cut into one half of a potato, with all the
colours painted on at the same time, to allow one-step printing.
A row of potato stamps like this has a three-dimensional quality,
which is enhanced by the choice and positioning of the colours.

YOU WILL NEED
♦ *ruler*
♦ *potato*
♦ *felt-tipped pen*
♦ *scalpel*
♦ *knife*
♦ *gouache, poster or acrylic paint in red,*
light blue, dark blue, green and yellow
♦ *paintbrush*

1 Measure the width of the shelf edge and cut the potato to fit. Copy the pattern shape from the template section on to the potato. Cut down with a scalpel to outline the shape, then cut across with a knife to scoop away the background.

2 Mix the paint, if necessary, then apply each colour to a separate part of the design with a paintbrush.

3 Begin printing along the shelf edge, making the first print on the short side section that will be nearest the wall.

4 Continue to apply the paint as before and stamp the pattern to cover all the shelf edges.

FISH FOOTSTOOL

This low stool decorated with a leaping fish motif would look good in the bathroom or on the patio for drinks,
or it could be used simply for putting your feet up.
Any small and useful stool that looks handmade would be a suitable candidate for a make-over.
The fish and border blocks are cut from high-density foam and the light and dark blue patterns are reminiscent
of Balinese batik prints.

YOU WILL NEED

- *small stool*
- *emulsion paint in dark blue, light blue and off-white*
- *paintbrushes*
- *tracing paper*
- *pencil*
- *scalpel*
- *spray adhesive*
- *high-density foam, such as upholstery foam*
- *scrap paper*
- *plate*

1 Give the stool two coats of dark blue paint and leave to dry. Trace, transfer and cut out the pattern shapes from the template section. Lightly spray the shapes with adhesive and place them on the foam. Cut around the outlines with a scalpel then scoop out the pattern details.

2 Print five fish shapes on to paper and cut them out. Use these to plan the position of the fish on the stool.

3 Spread some light blue and off-white paint on a plate. Using a paintbrush, apply off-white paint to the top of the fish and light blue to the bottom half. Make a test print to ensure that the stamp is not overloaded.

4 Using the paper markers as a guide, stamp the fish lightly on the surface of the stool, printing both colours at the same time.

5 Paint the border stamp using the off-white paint. The border is intentionally ragged, so don't go for strict straight edges, but stamp the design in a slightly haphazard fashion.

EGYPTIAN TABLE-TOP

The beauty of this table-top design lies in its simplicity. Just one colour was used on a bold background, with three similar images stamped in regimented rows. The table used here has a lower shelf, but the design would work equally well on any occasional table.

The salmon-pink prints show up well on the rich background, making it look even bluer. The stamps are pre-cut and are taken from Ancient Egyptian hieroglyphs. The finished table could be one element of a themed room, or the surprising and eye-catching centrepiece of a room decorated in subdued colours.

YOU WILL NEED

- ◆ 3 hieroglyphic rubber stamps
- ◆ ruler
- ◆ 2 card strips, for measuring stamp positions
- ◆ felt-tipped pen
- ◆ set square
- ◆ emulsion or acrylic paint in salmon-pink
- ◆ small paint roller
- ◆ piece of card or plastic

1 Use the stamp blocks and a ruler to measure out the stamp positions. Place a card strip along the vertical edge of the table. Mark as many stamp lengths as will fit along it, leaving equal spaces between them. Work out the positioning carefully so that the rows of prints will fit comfortably. Use the second card strip to mark the widths of the stamps.

2 Place the horizontal measure across the table so that it marks the position of the first row. The top of the stamp will touch the measuring strip. Use a set square to position the vertical strip at a 90-degree angle to the first row. Move the vertical strip along as you stamp. Coat the roller with paint by running it through a blob of paint on a spare piece of card or plastic.

3 Use the roller to coat the stamps, then print them in sequence all along the first row. Position the stamps following the marks you have made on the card strips.

4 Move the horizontal measure up one stamp space on the vertical measure and stamp a second row of figures. Once again, the tops of the stamps will touch the bottom of the horizontal strip. Check that the card measures remain at a 90-degree angle. Continue until the pattern covers the whole table-top.

FABRICS

MAKING PATTERNS on fabric with rubber or foam stamps is not a new idea and many textiles from small rural communities are still handblocked today. At the other end of the market, very expensive, limited editions of "designer" textiles gain their value because of their labour-intensive style of production.

There are a few important rules to obey with fabric: always wash it first; always use permanent inks (some need heat-sealing); and always work with a protective backing sheet under the fabric. Some fabrics have special surfaces, to resist staining for instance, and they will not absorb the ink. Other fabrics to avoid are very loose weaves and furry materials. Fabric conditioner and starch will affect the ink's performance, so avoid them if you are pre-washing some fabric for printing.

There are fabric inks available especially for rubber stamps, either in inkpad form or in applicator bottles. It is not strictly necessary to use fabric paint when stamping with foam or potato cuts, but you should check the colour fastness of any alternative paint. Consistency is also important: too much runny fabric paint will spread as you print, and paint that is too dry, or fast-drying, will not be absorbed and will flake off. The advantage of using inks specifically designed for fabric is that the consistency will be right and the results guaranteed. If, however, you are working on a wall hanging or mat that will not be washed, you can print with any substance that gives the desired results.

Another method of fabric printing is to stamp the patterns on paper and then transfer them to the fabric with a hot iron. Transfer ink comes in a range of colours and is available from specialist rubber-stamp dealers. This method works well on small projects but would be tedious on longer lengths of fabric, like curtaining, as it involves double the work, and the whole point of stamping is its wonderful instant results.

FABRIC APPLICATION

There are several types of fabric ink suitable for stamp printing - the two main types are those used to stamp directly on to fabric and those which are stamped on to paper first and then heat-transferred. The inks used in these samples are all stamped directly, but you can see transfer printing in the scarf project in this chapter.

Although these prints have all been made with fabric printing ink, different methods of application have been used. Some stamps are more successful than others, but all produce their own distinctive effects.

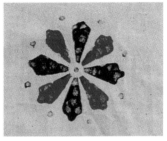

This print was made by inking a high-density foam stamp in two colours.

These prints were made with wine bottle corks with bored holes.

This print was made by inking a high-density foam stamp in a single colour.

This high-density foam stamp was inked in blue with a halo of red dots.

This fleur-de-lis print was made with a high-density foam stamp and red fabric ink for a crisp, intense finish.

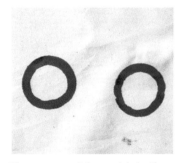

These potato-cut circles were inked with two colours to create an irregular pattern.

This print was made with a potato cut.

This print was made with a sponge stamp.

This print was made with a rubber stamp.

AUTUMNAL BED LINEN

Matching bed linen is the last word in luxury. The white pillow-cases have an all-round border of horse chestnuts and leaves and the top sheet folds back to reveal a matching pattern. Smooth cotton with straight edging is a dream to work on, because the stamps can be confidently lined up with the edges and the sheeting absorbs the ink well to give a very crisp print.

The fabric stamping ink comes in an applicator bottle, so it can be applied directly on to the stamp. Follow the manufacturer's instructions to make the pattern permanent - the ink works equally well on polycotton sheeting.

YOU WILL NEED

- ◆ rubber stamp
- ◆ fabric stamping ink in dark green and blue
- ◆ scrap paper
- ◆ scissors
- ◆ sheet and pillow-case
- ◆ sheet of thin card

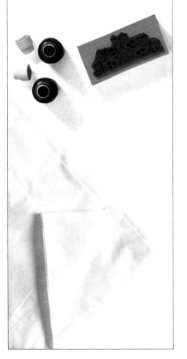

1 In order to plan your design, stamp out several motifs on to scrap paper and cut them out. Arrange these along the sheet edge or the pillow-case border to work out the final position and spacing of your pattern.

2 Place a sheet of card under the sheet, or inside the pillow-case, to prevent the ink soaking through.

3 Following the manufacturer's instructions, apply green ink to half of the stamp.

4 Apply blue ink to the other half of the stamp.

5 Test the distribution of the ink by making a print on to a scrap of fabric. Re-apply and test the ink until you feel confident enough to make the first print on to the fabric.

6 Check the arrangement of the paper-stamped motifs, then lift one at a time and stamp the fabric in its place. Press quite firmly, to give the fabric time to absorb the ink.

7 Continue to re-ink and test the stamp as you print all the way around the edges to complete a matching bed linen set. Finally, follow the fabric ink manufacturer's instructions to make the border permanent.

NO-SEW STAR CURTAIN

This is a quick and stylish solution to window dressing, especially if you don't like sewing. Light muslin drapes beautifully and its transparency allows the star pattern to show through the gathered layers. The motif is cut from medium-density sponge which is quite absorbent and makes several prints before you need to re-charge your sponge stamp.

You can use gold fabric paint but a more brilliant, glittering result is achieved by mixing bronze powder into a PVA glue and water base.

YOU WILL NEED

- ♦ pencil
- ♦ tracing paper
- ♦ scalpel
- ♦ spray adhesive
- ♦ felt-tipped pen
- ♦ medium-density sponge, such as a kitchen sponge
- ♦ bowl
- ♦ PVA glue
- ♦ bronze powder
- ♦ paintbrush
- ♦ plate
- ♦ sheet of paper, the width of the muslin
- ♦ white butter muslin

1 Trace, transfer and cut out the pattern shape from the template section. Lightly spray the shape with adhesive and place it on the sponge. Draw around it with felt-tipped pen.

2 Cut out the shape with a scalpel. First cut around the outline, then part the sponge and cut all the way through.

3 Mix up the gold colour in a bowl, using two spoons of PVA glue to one spoon of water and half a spoon of bronze powder. You can make a large or small amount of the mixture, just keep the proportions the same. Spread an even coating of the gold mixture on to a plate.

4 Place the paper underneath the muslin. Make a test print to ensure that the sponge is not overloaded, then print the first star just in from the corner. Measure the position of the next stamp with the width of three or four splayed fingers.

5 Measure upwards in the same way, and make the first star of the second row. This should be evenly spaced between the first two stars on the first row. Continue in this way, alternating the two rows, until you have covered the fabric with evenly spaced stars.

SPRIGGED CALICO CURTAINS

Natural calico has a lovely creamy colour, especially when the sun shines through it. However, it is usually
used as an upholsterer's lining fabric and this association can make calico curtains look unfinished. This
stamped floral sprig lifts the humble calico into another dimension, giving it a sophisticated finish.
Calico is prone to shrinkage, so wash the fabric before you stamp it and make up the curtains.
Refer to the section at the beginning of the book for instructions for making linocut stamps.
You will find the pattern in the template section.

YOU WILL NEED
♦ *calico fabric*
♦ *linocut stamp*
♦ *scrap paper*
♦ *fabric stamping ink in green and*
dark blue
♦ *scalpel*
♦ *ruler*
♦ *card*
♦ *pencil*

1 Lay the fabric out on a flat surface, such as a wallpaper-pasting table. Make several prints of the linocut stamp on scrap paper, cut these out with a scalpel and use them to plan the position of the motifs on the fabric.

2 Decide on the distance between the sprigs and cut out a square of card with the same dimensions to act as a measuring guide. Use it diagonally, making a pencil mark at each corner over the surface of the fabric.   ➤

3 Apply green ink directly to the edges of the linocut stamp.

4 Fill in the middle of the stamp with dark blue ink. Make an initial print on a scrap of fabric to determine the density of the stamped image.

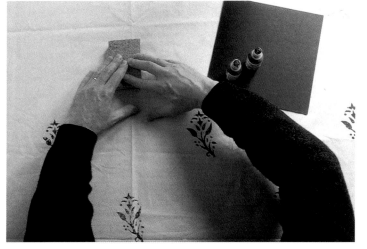

▲ *Calico tie-backs can be made to match the main fabric. You may find it easier to make the tie-back before stamping, to determine the best position for the design.*

5 Stamp the floral sprig on to the calico, using the pencil marks to position the base of the stamp. You need to apply gentle pressure to the back of the stamp and allow a couple of seconds for the ink to transfer. Don't rush; the result will be all the better for the extra time taken.

STELLAR TABLECLOTH

These rubber stamps are the perfect way to add a heavenly aspect to your dining table, and it could not be easier to achieve. Fabric or paper napkins can be stamped to match the tablecloth.

The tablecloth used here has a scalloped edge which makes for very easy spacing - simply count the scallops and then decide to stamp on, say, every third one. If you have a straight-edged cloth, measure the length and width of the cloth, and the length and width of the stamp to discover how many would fit comfortably along the edge. If the cloth isn't very big, find the centre by folding in half and then in half again. Begin with a stamp at each corner, then one at the halfway mark, and space the others in between.

YOU WILL NEED
- ♦ *tablecloth and napkins*
- ♦ *large and small star rubber stamps*
- ♦ *fabric stamping ink in navy blue*

1 Plan the position of your motifs, using one of the methods described above. Coat the smaller stamp with fabric ink and make a test print on to a scrap of fabric to ensure that the stamp is not overloaded.

2 Make the first print by positioning a small star in one corner.

85

3 Stamp a large star on either side of it and continue along the edges, alternating the sizes of the stars.

4 Stamp one widely spaced square of small stars approximately 10cm/4in in from the first row (depending upon the size of your cloth) and then another square of large stars another 10cm/4in closer to the centre. It should look like an all-over pattern with a border.

◄ *Scalloped edges and geometric stars create a contemporary look for a dining-room or occasional table.*

AFRICAN-STYLE CUSHIONS

This glorious pile of cushions is a real stamper's fashion statement. The fabulous animal motifs create a distinctive African look. The stamps are perfect for making a themed, but not identical, set of cushions to display together.
The covers are made from rough homespun fabric that has been vegetable dyed in rich, spicy shades. The combination of the primitive stamped shapes and the textured fabric is very effective.

YOU WILL NEED

♦ *fabric-stamping ink in black*
♦ *3 African-style rubber stamps*
♦ *loose-weave cushion covers*
♦ *sheet of card*

1 Apply the fabric ink directly to the stamp and make a test print on a scrap of fabric to ensure that the stamp is not overloaded.

2 Place a sheet of card inside the cover to protect the other side.

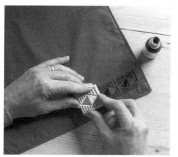

3 Re-ink the stamp and print a row of small motifs round the edges to create a border.

4 Stamp a row of the larger motif at even intervals above the border. Use a combination of all three stamps in this way to complete the cushion design. Arrange the stamps in different ways on the other covers, either radiating out from the centre, or forming circles and squares.

TRAIL-BLAZER SCARF

*Beginners are often nervous about printing on fabric for the first time. Here is a no-risk method of fabric-
printing which allows you to make all the design decisions and complete the stamping before you go near the
fabric. The stamp is inked with fabric-transfer colour and the pattern laid out on paper first. The paper is then
placed face-down on the fabric and a light pressure is applied to the back with a heated iron. When the paper
is removed, the design will be transferred to the fabric in reverse.
If you are still hesitant, rest assured that the printing must be done on synthetic fabric,
so the project is relatively inexpensive.*

YOU WILL NEED
- ◆ *scarf in synthetic fabric*
- ◆ *thin white paper*
- ◆ *scissors*
- ◆ *3 different rubber stamps*
- ◆ *transfer inkpads in red, blue and green*

1 Measure the width of the scarf and
cut paper strips of the same length.
Make a border along each paper strip,
using two alternating stamps in red
and blue. You will need four borders.

2 Cut a piece of paper to fit in the
central area of the scarf. Stamp a
widely spaced pattern using the third
stamp and green ink.

3 Place the scarf on a flat surface and
turn the stamped paper borders face-
down in position along the edges.

4 Apply light pressure with a dry iron. Follow the manufacturer's instructions on timing and temperature. Lift the iron between motifs – a sliding iron will blur your print.

5 Transfer the central pattern with the iron in the same way.

CHINA & GLASS

STAMPING A MOTIF gives the same print every time and this will enable you to make matching sets of crockery and glassware.

Several brands of paint on the market are designed to be used on these surfaces at home. They don't need firing in kilns at high temperatures, but the paint can be made more resilient by baking in a domestic oven. The one drawback is that this paint is not recommended for food use, which means avoiding mouth contact, so don't paint around the lip of a glass or cup. If you choose to do the tea set project, we suggest you follow the paint manufacturer's guidelines or use it as a display set.

Ceramic paints or acrylic enamels make good, crisp, opaque prints which are particularly effective on clear glass. Many foodstuffs are packed in glass, and stamping is a perfect way to turn the jars from kitchen waste into kitchen accessories.

If you are planning to tile the bathroom or kitchen, you will probably know how expensive hand-decorated tiles can be. Specialist paints and stamps offer an alternative. Tiles can be decorated and oven-baked before being applied to the wall in an arrangement with plain tiles. They are best used where heavy soiling is unlikely because, tough as they are, they won't stand up to abrasive cleaning with powerful detergents.

Apart from the projects featured there are many other ways to use the paints and stamps: ceramic lamp bases; candlesticks; windows and door knobs, for example. These projects are just the beginning - once you have realized the possibilities for decorating glassware and ceramics, there will be no stopping you!

CERAMIC AND GLASS APPLICATION

Different surfaces bring out the different qualities of paint. The kind of stamp used will also have a big influence on the final result. To illustrate the different effects that can be achieved, we have used the same motif, cut from rubber, foam and potato, with a variety of inks, paints and stains. Some choices may seem unusual, like woodstain on terracotta, but experimentation can produce unexpected successes!

The left print on the rim was made with emulsion paint applied with a sponge.

The central print on the pot was made with wood dye applied with a sponge.

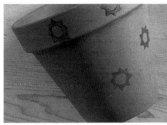

The central print on the pot was made with tinted varnish applied with a rubber stamp.

The central print on the rim was made with emulsion paint applied with a rubber stamp.

The central print on the pot was made with wood dye applied with a potato cut.

The central print on the rim was made with tinted varnish applied with a potato cut.

These prints were made with acrylic enamel paint and applied with (left) a potato cut, (right) a sponge, and (below) a rubber stamp.

This print was made with a coil of foam dipped into emulsion paint. The emulsion was left to dry and then covered with a protective coat of clear varnish.

These prints were made with acrylic enamel paint thinned with clear acrylic varnish, applied with (top left) a sponge, (lower left) a potato cut, and (right) a rubber stamp.

TILE APPLICATION

These are just a small selection of the different effects that can be achieved by stamp printing on to tiles. We recommend that you always use acrylic enamel paints, and wherever possible, decorate them before you put them on a wall because this gives you the chance to add to their resilience by baking them in the oven. Always follow manufacturer's instructions for times and temperatures and ensure your tiles can withstand this treatment.

These little circles were made by dipping bored wine bottle corks into red and blue paint, and printing in rows.

These larger circles were made using a potato cut. The transparent effect comes from the potato starch mixing in with the paint, and the way in which the smooth potato disperses the paint.

This print was made with a shaped, medium-density sponge. The textured effect is due to the density of the sponge.

This pattern was made using small rubber stamps cut from an eraser. A zigzag pattern like this makes a good border.

This heart was cut from medium-density sponge and the textured effect is opaque but "powdery"

This plaid pattern was made by dipping straight strips of high-density foam into red and blue paint. The thickness of the strips can be varied to produce a tartan pattern.

A small square of foam was used to print this chequerboard effect. This pattern is quite time-consuming, but very effective.

This high-density foam stamp was coloured with a brush to make a three-colour print. These prints make good highlights when mixed in with single-colour stamp prints.

This border was made with a medium-density foam block, printed in different colours. The edges must be aligned accurately for best effect.

FLEUR-DE-LIS TILES

This enduring heraldic motif has recently undergone one of its many popular revivals and features on anything from carpets and curtains to dinner plates and biscuit tins. The symbol originated in the twelfth century when the French king Louis VII chose it as his crusading symbol.
The fleur-de-lis used here was cut from high-density foam and used with acrylic enamel paint. The paint can be fired in a conventional oven, following the manufacturer's instructions. This will make it strong enough to be wiped down with mild cleaning solution, but not tough enough to withstand abrasive cleaning fluids.

YOU WILL NEED

- *tracing paper*
- *pencil*
- *spray adhesive*
- *high-density foam, such as upholstery foam*
- *scalpel*
- *acrylic enamel paint in black and blue*
- *plate*
- *paintbrush*
- *plain white tiles*

1 Trace and transfer the pattern shape from the template section. Lightly spray the shape with adhesive and place it on the foam.

2 Use a scalpel to cut around the outline of the fleur-de-lis, then across to scoop away the background.

3 Cut away the edges of the foam, so that the block has the outline of the motif - this will make positioning much easier.

4 Spread an even coating of black paint on to a plate, and mix in enough blue to lighten the colour. ➤

5 Dip the foam block into the paint, then make a test print on scrap paper to ensure that the stamp is not overloaded.

6 Position the stamp in the middle of the tile, on the diagonal, then press it lightly to make the print.

7 Lift the stamp straight up from the surface without moving it sideways, which would blur the print.

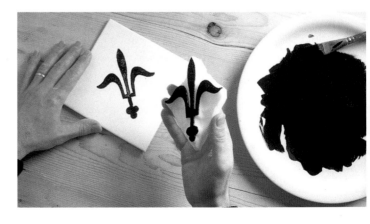

STAR-STRUCK TEA SERVICE

If you are bored with your plain teacups and saucers, why not cheer yourself up with some
pretty stamped patterns in vibrant colours?
Glazed china can be painted with special acrylic enamel paint that achieves a higher level of permanence
when baked in a domestic oven. Although the manufacturers of this type of paint stress that it is not
for food use, it can be used on crockery as long as the decoration is kept away from the drinking edges
of cups and confined to the outside of bowls and plates. Washing should be gentle; on no account
should decorated crockery be put into a dishwasher.

YOU WILL NEED
- ◆ *pencil*
- ◆ *tracing paper*
- ◆ *scalpel*
- ◆ *spray adhesive*
- ◆ *eraser*
- ◆ *acrylic enamel paints in orange, blue and black*
- ◆ *small sheet of glass*
- ◆ *paintbrush*
- ◆ *plain white china tea service*

1 Trace, transfer and cut out the pattern shape from the template section. Lightly spray the shape with adhesive and stick it on to the end of an eraser.

2 Cut around the outline of the star with a scalpel, making sure that the points are sharp.

3 Cut horizontally into the eraser, to meet the outline cuts and remove the excess. The star shape must have points of even lengths – make a test print, and adjust any obvious flaws with the scalpel before you begin on the china.

4 Spread an even coating of orange paint on to the glass and press the star stamp into it. Make a test print to ensure that the stamp is not overloaded, then begin stamping widely spaced orange stars. The inked stamp will tend to slide on the glazed surface, so compensate for this by dotting it on, and removing it directly.

5 Stamp the blue stars in the same way, leaving space for the final colour.

6 Stamp the black stars so that the three colours form an all-over pattern. Bake the china in the oven, following the manufacturer's instructions on temperature and timing.

JAPANESE-STYLE GLASS VASE

Transform a plain glass vase with some chic calligraphic stamping.
For this project, high-density foam was cut into strips, then dipped into acrylic enamel paint. The strips were
then twisted into different shapes to make a series of quick prints. Don't make too many prints - the end result
should look like an enlargement of a Japanese calligraphic symbol.
The paint finish is tough enough to withstand gentle washing, but take care, because all unfired surface
decoration such as this is prone to chipping and peeling.

YOU WILL NEED

♦ *set square*
♦ *felt-tipped pen*
♦ *high-density foam, such as*
upholstery foam, 25cm x 10cm x 5cm/
10in x 4in x 2in
♦ *scalpel*
♦ *kitchen cloth*
♦ *plain glass vase*
♦ *acrylic enamel paint in black*
♦ *plate*

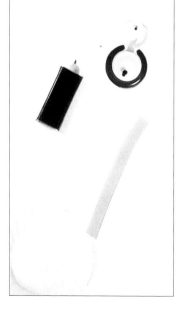

1 Using a set square and felt-tipped pen, draw lines 1cm/½in apart along the length of the foam.

2 Cut along the lines using a scalpel, then part the foam and cut all the way through it.

3 Clean the vase thoroughly with a kitchen cloth to remove any surface grease and dry it well.

4 Spread an even coating of paint on to a plate. Curl up a strip of foam and dip it into the paint.

5 Use both hands, positioned just above the glass surface, to curl the foam strip into an open-ended shape. When the curve looks right, press it on to the vase. Lift it off straight away to avoid any smudging.

6 Press a straight strip of foam into the paint then use it to continue the line around the side of the vase.

7 Complete the calligraphic pattern with a series of these straight black lines. Applying the pressure unevenly will give a more authentic effect.

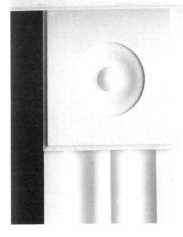

SNOWFLAKE STORAGE JARS

*Almost every kitchen could do with the occasional face-lift. Rather than pay for a completely new look, why
not just cheer up your storage jars and give your kitchen a breath of fresh air?
You can create a whole new atmosphere by stamping patterns on your jars with acrylic enamel paint. The
finish is quite tough and will stand up to occasional gentle washing, but will not withstand the dishwasher.
Choose a design that suits your kitchen, or copy the pattern for the motif used here.*

YOU WILL NEED
♦ *pencil*
♦ *tracing paper*
♦ *spray adhesive*
♦ *high-density foam, such as
upholstery foam*
♦ *scalpel*
♦ *kitchen cloth*
♦ *glass storage jars*
♦ *acrylic enamel paint in white*
♦ *plate*
♦ *tile*

1 Trace and transfer the pattern shape
from the template section. Lightly
spray the shape with adhesive and
place it on the foam. Cut around the
outline with a scalpel.

2 Cut horizontally into the foam to
meet the outline cuts and remove the
excess foam.

3 Clean the glass jars thoroughly with
a kitchen cloth, then dry them well.

This will remove any surface grease
and will provide a better surface.

4 Spread an even coating of paint on to a plate. Press the stamp into it and make a test print on a tile to ensure that the stamp is not overloaded.

5 Holding the jar steady with your spare hand, press the flexible foam stamp around the side of the jar.

6 Rotate the stamp 90 degrees and make the second print directly below the first. Continue in this way, alternating the angle of the print.

PERSONALIZED FLOWERPOTS

*Commercially decorated flowerpots can be very expensive but you can customize ordinary clay pots
very easily - and the designs will be uniquely yours.
The sunwheel motif used here is an ancient symbol with real energy. The colours chosen create a vibrant
display that is best complemented by bright, attractive pot plants. Change the plants according to
the season or to suit your mood.
Three sponges, three colours of paint and a roll of masking tape are all you need to turn plain flowerpots
into a sensational display.*

YOU WILL NEED

♦ *pencil*
♦ *tracing paper*
♦ *scalpel*
♦ *spray adhesive*
♦ *high-density foam, such as
upholstery foam*
♦ *acrylic enamel paint in navy blue,
red and cream*
♦ *3 plates*
♦ *glazed and plain terracotta flowerpots*
♦ *masking tape*

1 Trace, transfer and cut out the
pattern shapes from the template
section. Lightly spray the shapes with
adhesive and place them on the foam.

2 Use a scalpel to cut around the
outlines of the large motif. Scoop out
the background and the pattern
details.

3 Cut out the small motif in the
same way.

4 Spread an even coating of navy blue
paint on to a plate and press the large
motif into it. Make a test print to
ensure that the stamp is not
overloaded.

106

5 Stamp the large motif around the pot four times.

6 Spread an even coating of red paint on to a plate and press the small motif into it. Make a test print to ensure the stamp is not overloaded. Stamp the small motif in groups above and below the large ones.

7 Cut out a small stepped triangle from foam using a scalpel.

8 Place two parallel strips of masking tape around the top end of a blue glazed flowerpot. Leave a 1cm/½in gap between the two strips.

9 Squeeze some cream paint on to a plate. With an off cut of sponge, apply the paint to the gap between the masking tape strips.

10 Allow time for the paint to dry and then peel off the masking tape to reveal the cream border around the top of the pot.

11 Ensure the cream paint is spread evenly on a plate. Press the stepped triangle shape into it. Make a test print first, then stamp the pattern above and below the cream line, matching up the points of the triangle.

Accessories

ACCESSORIES are probably the ideal starting-point if
you have never considered a rubber stamp as a decorating tool. You can transform a lampshade, picture frame
or wooden tray in minutes, with minimal effort and
even less mess. All you need is a stamp and an inkpad
to create an all-over pattern, then a quick rinse with
water to clean the stamp. What could be easier?

Starting a new craft activity is often the most
difficult part, so it makes sense to begin with something small, until you have built up the confidence to
attempt more ambitious projects. This shouldn't take
long, because stamping is so easy and so little can go
wrong. Stamping is a compulsive activity, partly
because it is so quick but mostly because it is so
effective - just one strong design can enliven the most
ordinary object.

A good starting-point is the gift-wrapping paper; all
you need is a bought rubber stamp with a coloured
inkpad and a sheet of plain paper. You will be amazed
at how good the paper will look, even with the most
basic arrangement of the stamps in rows. Experiment
with colours and groups of stamps, and before long you
will be collecting other stamps to try different designs.

Many commercially bought rubber stamps are
particularly suited to small objects, as their fine details
might get lost on a large area such as a wall or
bedcover. Once you have explored their potential you
may want to design your own. You can give your
design to a stamp manufacturer for a custom-made
rubber stamp, but this can be quite expensive. Unless
you know you will be using the design over and over
again, you might want to carve your own. Carved
erasers will give a real rubber stamp effect, and as they
are fairly inexpensive you can practise and perfect your
motif to create something really original.

STYLISH LAMPSHADE

Unusual lampshades can be very expensive. The solution is to take a plain lampshade and apply some surface decoration that will transform it from a utility object into a stylish focal point.
The design, which resembles a seedpod, is easy to cut from high-density foam. It makes a bold, sharp-edged print and the flexibility of the foam means that it can bend around the curved surface.
Remember to extend the pattern beyond the edges of the lampshade, so that only parts of the motifs appear. The lampshade will look as if it has been made from handprinted fabric.

YOU WILL NEED

♦ *pencil*
♦ *tracing paper*
♦ *spray adhesive*
♦ *high-density foam, such as upholstery foam*
♦ *scalpel*
♦ *thinned emulsion paint in creamy yellow and pale blue*
♦ *2 plates*
♦ *small rubber roller*
♦ *plain-coloured lampshade*

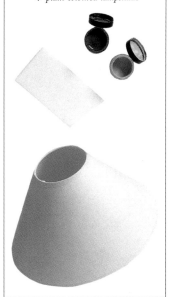

1 Trace and transfer the pattern shape from the template section. Lightly spray the shape with adhesive and place it on the foam. Cut out the motif using a scalpel. Cut around the outline first, going all the way through the foam. Cut around the centre detail to a depth of about 1cm/½in, then undercut and scoop out this section, and cut away the background.

2 Spread some creamy yellow paint on to a plate and coat a small roller evenly. Use it to apply a coating of paint to the stamp.

3 Make the first print a partial one, using only the top end of the stamp. Continue to print at random angles, leaving plenty of spaces for the second colour. Wash the stamp, removing all traces of yellow.

4 Spread some pale blue paint on a second plate and coat the roller. Use it to apply an even coating of paint to the stamp.

5 Stamp blue shapes at random angles in between the yellow ones. Be sure to make some partial prints so that the pattern continues over the edges.

ABSTRACT TRAY DESIGN

Household trays are ideal objects for trying out new designs and new paint effects. They are relatively cheap so if you are not happy with the end result it doesn't really matter. On the other hand, if you like your design, you have a bold, bright accessory that you can use every day.
The sponges have been cut into an assortment of angular shapes and stamped on in three colours. Preserve the freshness of this pattern by applying at least three coats of clear varnish to protect your tray from tea, coffee and other stains.

YOU WILL NEED

♦ *emulsion or gouache paint in cream*
♦ *paintbrushes*
♦ *felt-tipped pen*
♦ *medium-density sponge, such as a kitchen sponge*
♦ *scalpel*
♦ *scissors*
♦ *small amounts of emulsion or gouache paint in olive-green, brick-red and grey*
♦ *3 plates*
♦ *clear varnish*

1 Apply two coats of cream emulsion or gouache paint to the whole tray. Leave to dry between coats.

2 Copy the pattern shapes from the template section on to the sponge surface in felt-tipped pen. Use a scalpel and sharp scissors to cut out the nine shapes. They should look spontaneous; do not be too worried about cutting out precisely.

3 Spread an even coating of olive-green paint on to a plate. Choose a shape and, having first made a test print, make a print on the tray.

4 Use about half of the shapes with the olive-green paint, printing randomly all over the tray surfaces. Press lightly to leave a textured effect.

5 Spread an even coating of brick-red paint on to a plate and print in the same way as before, using the rest of the shapes. Leave some gaps for the final colour.

6 Spread the grey paint on to a plate and use a combination of all the shapes to fill in any spaces in the pattern. It should cover the inside and outside of the tray. Let some of the shapes overlap the edges, to make partial prints.

7 When the paint is dry, finish the tray with at least three coats of clear varnish, allowing sufficient drying time between each coat.

PAINTERLY PORTFOLIO

Protect your priceless works of art in this stylishly stamped portfolio. The varying density of the potato prints creates a suitably painterly effect.

The portfolio is made from two sheets of thick mounting board with an edge-binding of broad, black woven tape. An authentic finishing touch is added by threading black tape through slits in both sides and using it to tie the portfolio together.

The project can be made any size and would make an ideal stationery folder.

YOU WILL NEED

- ◆ knife
- ◆ medium to large potato
- ◆ pair of compasses
- ◆ scalpel
- ◆ plate
- ◆ gouache paint in Prussian-blue
- ◆ paintbrush
- ◆ 2 sheets light blue mounting board
- ◆ broad black woven adhesive tape
- ◆ black cloth tape, 1cm/½in wide cut into 2 x 20cm/8in lengths

1 Cut the potato in half. Use the pair of compasses to draw two circles on the potato half, one inside the other. They should form a ring, about 6mm/¼in thick with an inner diameter of 6cm/2½in.

2 Cut around the outline with a scalpel. Scoop out the middle and cut away the excess on the outer edge.

3 Spread an even coating of Prussian-blue gouache paint on to a plate. Apply the paint to the potato design with a paintbrush.

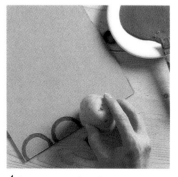

4 Beginning at the edge nearest you, overlap half the potato to print a row of half-circles to start the pattern off.

7 Cut two strips of adhesive tape 4cm/1½in longer than the height of the card. Lay one, sticky side up, on a flat surface then drop the two sides of the portfolio into position. Leave a gap between them and an overlap top and bottom.

5 Stamp the next row of prints to fit between the rings on the first row. Carry on until you have covered the board completely.

6 Overprint another layer of circles. Vary the amount and density of the paint when you stamp to create an attractive handmade look.

8 Place the second strip of adhesive tape over the join on the inside of the portfolio, and trim its ends level with the board.

9 Fold down the excess tape from the outside, top and bottom, to give a neat finish.

10 Cut a 1.5cm/⅝in slit in each side of the portfolio, halfway down and 3cm/1¼in in from the outside edge. Thread the black cloth tape through,

leaving 2.5cm/1in to secure it on the inside. Stick a neat square of black adhesive tape over the ends of the cloth tape.

BOHEMIAN BOOK COVERS

Brown parcel paper is perfect book-covering material - it is strong, folds crisply and costs very little. The paper usually has a shiny side and a matt side, with the matt side more absorbent to paint.

Pattern making with potato cuts is great fun, and the elements used here - a small solid square, a square outline, and a triangle - can be used in different combinations to make a variety of designs. These papers would make ideal covers for a row of cookbooks on a kitchen shelf.

The watercolour paint is mixed with PVA glue which dries transparent, leaving a slight sheen that looks great combined with the characteristic potato-cut texture.

YOU WILL NEED

- ♦ *knife*
- ♦ *2 potatoes*
- ♦ *bowl*
- ♦ *PVA glue*
- ♦ *paintbrush*
- ♦ *watercolour paint in brick-red, brown and yellow-ochre*
- ♦ *plate*
- ♦ *scalpel*
- ♦ *brown parcel paper*

1 Cut the potatoes in half, then trim the edges to give them all the same square shape.

2 In a bowl mix PVA glue and water in equal amounts, then add a drop of watercolour paint. The texture should be thick and sticky.

3 Spread an even coating of the paint mixture on to a plate then dip a potato into it - this will make it easier to see the design as you cut it out. Leave a square border around the edge, then divide the rest of the surface diagonally. Scoop out one triangular section with a scalpel.

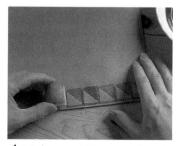

4 Print a row of this pattern along the bottom edge of the paper.

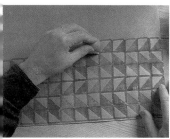

5 Stamp the following row with the same stamp the other way up. Add variety to the design by rotating the stamp for each new row, to form different patterns.

6 To make a chequerboard pattern, leave a gap between the prints. Dip a small piece of potato into the paint and stamp dots in the middle of the blank squares. Experiment with your own combinations.

GLORIOUS GIFTWRAP

If you want to make a gift extra special, why not print your own wrapping paper, designed to suit the person to whom you are giving the present? All you need is a selection of rubber stamps, inkpads or paint, and plain paper. Your homemade giftwrap will show that you really wanted to make the gift memorable. Stamped paper is great at Christmas when you need to wrap lots of presents at the same time. Your gifts will look very individual, so easy to recognize that you will be able to dispense with labels!

YOU WILL NEED
♦ *plain paper*
♦ *rubber stamps in a variety of motifs*
♦ *stamp inkpads*

1 To make a non-regimented design, like this clover-leaf pattern, first stamp at one edge of the paper. Then rotate the stamp in your hand to change the direction of each print. Re-charge the stamp with ink as required.

2 Turn the paper and continue stamping the shapes. The end result should have roughly an even amount of background to pattern.

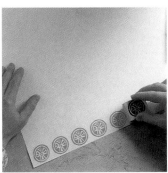

3 To achieve a more formal pattern, like this bird design, begin by stamping a row of shapes along the bottom edge.

4 Build up the design, alternating between two colours if you like, as shown here, to make an all-over pattern of closely spaced shapes.

PRIVATE CORRESPONDENCE

Personalized stationery makes a statement before you even put pen to paper. Although there are many ways of making your own stationery using pre-cut rubber stamps, this project goes one stage further and shows you how to make your own rubber stamp from an eraser. Choose one or two images that express something about your character to use on your writing paper.

You will need quite a high level of cutting skills because the stamp is a small one - you need patience and a steady hand. Once you get to grips with eraser carving you will be able to make your own intricate and long-lasting stamps with any design you choose.

YOU WILL NEED

- ◆ *drawings of your chosen motifs*
- ◆ *scalpel*
- ◆ *plain paper*
- ◆ *new eraser*
- ◆ *liquid lighter fuel*
- ◆ *lino-cutting tool*
- ◆ *stamp inkpad*
- ◆ *embossing ink and powder (optional)*

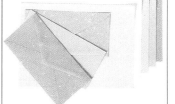

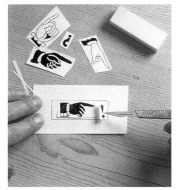

1 Cut out and arrange your chosen motifs on a piece of paper so they will fit on to the eraser.

2 Photocopy the arrangement of motifs and cut out the shape to fit the size of the eraser.

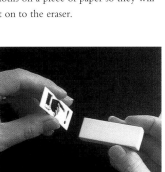

3 Place this squarely on the eraser, with the drawing face-down.

4 Spread about three drops of liquid lighter fuel over the back of the paper. Make sure the paper does not slide across the eraser as you do this. ➤

5 Remove the paper to reveal the transferred design. This will be reversed, but the stamping process will reverse it again, bringing it back to the original image.

6 Use a fine lino-cutting tool and a scalpel to cut around the outline and the pattern details carefully. Scoop out any excess to leave the design standing proud of the eraser - look at a pre-cut rubber stamp to judge the depth of the cut-away pieces.

1 Embossing kits are available from rubber stamp suppliers. To use, stamp your motif using embossing ink.

2 Sprinkle embossing powder over the ink (which will still be wet) and tap off the excess.

7 Press the eraser stamp into a coloured stamp inkpad and print your stationery. For a raised image, stamp the motif with embossing powder.

3 Follow the manufacturer's instructions to apply heat to the paper. This will produce a raised, glossy image.

CARDBOARD GIFT BOX

It is simple to transform a flat sheet of thin card into an attractive gift box. All you need is a ruler and a pencil to measure out the pattern accurately and a scalpel and straight edge to cut it out. The box edges are joined together with double-sided tape, which gives a strong, neat finish.
Stamp rows of scampering dogs diagonally across the box before folding it, to add a touch of frivolity. The box design can be scaled up or down, depending on the size you require, and the surface can be decorated with different stamped designs to suit the gift.

YOU WILL NEED

- ruler or set square
- pencil
- thin coloured card
- scalpel
- rubber stamp
- stamp inkpad
- blunt knife, for scoring the card
- double-sided tape

1 Draw out your box following the diagram in the template section. Increase or decrease the measurements as required, but keep the proportions the same.

2 Cut out the box, using a scalpel and ruler to make neat, accurate lines.

3 Using a straight edged piece of paper or ruler as a guide, stamp rows of motifs diagonally across the card.

4 It is important to extend the pattern over the edges, so stamp partial motifs at the ends of each alternate row.

5 On the wrong side of the card, hold a set square or ruler against the fold lines and score along them with a blunt knife. Do not break the surface of the card.

6 Fold along the score lines, making sure the corners are square. Apply double-sided tape to the joining edges, then peel off the backing paper and press the sides together. Accuracy is important at this stage, as double-sided tape cannot be re-positioned.

7 Continue folding and sticking the card in this way, ensuring the edges fit together neatly. Fold in the end pieces.

PRIMITIVE-STYLE FRAMES

Simple wooden frames can be transformed into a richly patterned, colour-matched set with
acrylic paint and pre-cut rubber stamps. The three frames used here are all different but have
enough in common to look great as a group.
Frames should not be too overbearing or they will outshine the pictures they are intended to display.
Use muted colour combinations like the ones chosen here, combined with geometric stamps
for an all-over pattern effect. When stamping a pattern of this type, make it texturally interesting
by varying the amount of paint used. Let the ink fade on some prints and be
almost blobby on others.

YOU WILL NEED
- ♦ *fine-grade sandpaper*
- ♦ *acrylic paint in sea-blue, sienna, stone and maize-yellow*
- ♦ *paintbrushes*
- ♦ *3 wooden frames*
- ♦ *3 plates*
- ♦ *3 rubber stamps*
- ♦ *clear matt varnish (optional)*

1 Follow the same procedure for all the frames, using different colours and rubber stamps. Sand down and paint each frame with acrylic. Leave to dry then apply a second coat for a really solid covering of colour.

2 Mix some sienna into the sea-blue to produce olive-green. Spread an even coating of the remaining colours on to separate plates.

3 Dip a stamp into the paint and make a test print on scrap paper to ensure that the stamp is not overloaded. Print closely-spaced motifs on to the background.

4 Stamp the design over every visible surface, going over the edges and around the sides. When the paint is dry, give each frame a coat of clear matt varnish if you wish.

CHILDREN'S ROOMS

CHILDREN GROW UP and change their ideas very quickly, so decorating on their behalf presents its own particular problems. Realistically you must expect them to demand a completely new decor around every five years. This can be quite liberating, however, as you don't have to think in the very long term; so throw caution to the wind and enjoy yourself. While the decor of their room might be important to some children, most - especially younger ones - will be happy for you to make the decorating decisions for them.

The rooms shown in the projects are a tropical bathroom, a playroom mural, a quilt-style frieze and a spotted room for an older child. The bathroom is the easiest as it requires no preparation at all. You just dip and stamp - the more energetic you are, the better. The other projects do require some planning and preparation, but once the measuring is out of the way, the stamping is over almost too quickly.

For the tree mural, a sponge is used like a brush before the foliage is stamped on. The result is a lovely, soft chalky effect with no hard edges. For an older child's room, what could be simpler than cutting a large spot from a piece of sponge? When this motif is used on a large scale it takes on a rather daring quality and is amazingly effective. Make the spots above the dado rail in one colour and below in another. As a variation a star stamp can be used between the spots in another colour.

Whether you are decorating for a baby, a young child or a young adult, these rooms should inspire you to look beyond bought borders and wallpapers. Decorate a room so that it is creative and individual.

SPOTTED BEDROOM WALLS

*Deciding on the bedroom decor for older children can sometimes be difficult. They are
definitely not babies and probably don't want a themed room. However, something light-hearted
and not too fussy can be hard to achieve.
A spot is the simplest of motifs and can be used on its own or in combination with other shapes.
Stars can be added as a variation, or darker spots stamped below the dado rail. The end result is far from
childish but neither is it too sombre. The colours used here are quite sophisticated but
another combination would change the mood completely.*

YOU WILL NEED

- ◆ *pair of compasses*
- ◆ *scrap paper*
- ◆ *scissors*
- ◆ *low-density sponge, such as a
  bath sponge*
- ◆ *felt-tipped pen*
- ◆ *scalpel*
- ◆ *emulsion paint in dusky blue*
- ◆ *plate*
- ◆ *plumb line*
- ◆ *ruler*
- ◆ *emulsion paint in black and yellow
  (optional)*

1 Use a pair of compasses to draw a circle with a diameter of 8cm/3¼in on scrap paper. Cut it out.

2 Use this circle as a template and draw two circles on the sponge with a felt-tipped pen.

3 Cut out the circles with a scalpel. First cut around the outline, then part the sponge and cut right through to the other side.

4 If you are using the stars with the spots, draw out a star shape on the sponge and cut it out with a scalpel.

5 Spread an even coating of dusky blue emulsion on to a plate and press the spot stamp into it. Make a test print on to scrap paper to ensure that the stamp is not overloaded. If you trust your eye, then begin printing the spots in evenly spaced rows. If you need a guide, attach a plumb line at ceiling height and stamp the spots alongside it, measuring the distance between the spots with a ruler. Move the line along a measured distance and repeat the process.

6 For a more dramatic effect, darken the blue down a tone by adding some black, then stamp spots below the dado rail.

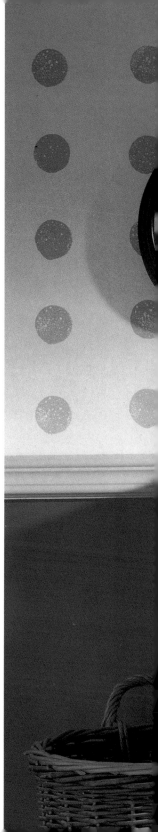

7 If you are using the star motif too, dip the sponge into yellow paint, test on scrap paper, and stamp stars at equal intervals between the spots. For further interest, you could mix a darker yellow, and stamp over the original stars, slightly off-centre, to create a drop shadow.

CARIBBEAN BATHROOM

Bathtime should be a fun-filled part of a child's day but sometimes there is a certain reluctance to enter the bathroom. Encourage your child by decorating the walls with bright and cheerful motifs.
This bathroom has a tropical seaside theme. The intense sky-blue of the background is separated from the sandy-yellow by a bright red peg rail, a feature that is both decorative and extremely functional.
The stamps are pre-cut bath sponges. We have copied the sponge colours here, but you could choose any colour combination you wished.

YOU WILL NEED
♦ emulsion paint in viridian-green, pink and yellow
♦ 3 plates
♦ set of tropical-theme sponges

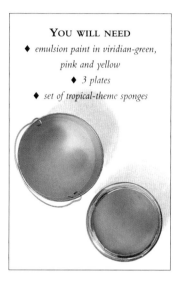

1 Spread even coatings of green, pink and yellow paint on to separate plates. Press the palm tree sponges into the green, then make a test print on scrap paper to ensure that the sponge is not overloaded with paint. Stamp the first print at a 45-degree angle, just above the peg rail.

2 Press the fish sponge into the pink paint and make a test print on scrap paper. Then stamp the fish beside the palm tree. Once again avoid an upright print, angle it slightly.

3 Press the pineapple sponge into the yellow paint, make a test print on paper, then stamp it above the others.

4 Continue stamping the three shapes until they fill the wall. Position the prints close to one another, and change the angle of the print each time so that the pattern is densely packed and completely random.

APPLE TREE MURAL

It is advisable to undertake this project when the children are out of the way. This sort of decorating is very appealing to young people and they will want to join in. However, if you are willing to let them help you, be prepared for a less stylish and more spontaneous result.

The apple tree mural is perfect for a playroom or for a new baby's room. It is the kind of design that will last throughout childhood, as it will not appear babyish too quickly.

The mural was painted with pieces of sponge instead of a brush to harmonize all the textures, so that the tree, leaves and fruit all have the same soft finish. The colours are muted to prevent the design becoming too overbearing.

YOU WILL NEED

♦ *stiff card*
♦ *pencil*
♦ *scalpel*
♦ *felt-tipped pen*
♦ *low-density sponge, such as a bath sponge*
♦ *diluted emulsion paint in pink, brick-red, yellow, sap-green, blue-grey, ochre and olive-green*
♦ *7 plates*
♦ *paintbrush*

1 Draw the branch, trunk and base shapes on to a sheet of stiff card. Cut out the shapes with a scalpel.

2 Draw a circle and a leaf on to the sponge and cut out the shapes. First cut around the outline, then part the sponge and cut right through.

3 Decide where to position the trees on the wall, and draw around the base template in pencil.

4 Draw the trunk above the base, using the long, rectangular template.

6 Spread the paint out on to separate plates with a paintbrush. For the base you will need pink, brick-red, yellow and sap-green. Starting at the skirting board, use a piece of sponge to fill in the pencil outline on the wall. Make a test print on scrap paper first to ensure the sponge is not overloaded.

5 Add six curved branches. Stagger three up one side, then flip the template over to draw three matching branches opposite them.

7 Fill in the tree trunk and the branches with the blue-grey paint. The sponging should not look perfect; it should be textured and rough. Cut the sponge into a point at one end to print the ends of the branches.

8 Stamp the leaves in ochre and olive-green. Overstamp one colour with the other occasionally, to give a three-dimensional effect.

9 Finally, use the sponge circle and pink paint to stamp the apples. Space them randomly in the foliage. Print some apples to overlap the leaves and print others partially, as if obscured by the leaves. Apply more pressure to one side of the sponge; it will print darker and give the fruit a shaded effect.

"COUNTRY QUILT" FRIEZE

Stamp this friendly, folk-style frieze in a child's bedroom in soft pinks and a warm green.
The pattern is reminiscent of an old-fashioned American appliqué quilt. The overlapping edges and
jauntily angled birds accentuate its naïve charm.
The colour scheme avoids the harshness of primaries which are so often chosen for children. Green is a calming
colour but it can be cold. For this project use a sap-green, which contains a lot of yellow, for warmth.
The finished effect is bright enough to be eye-catching without overpowering.

YOU WILL NEED

♦ emulsion or artist's acrylic paint in
sap-green, pink and crimson
♦ paintbrushes
♦ pencil
♦ ruler
♦ spirit level
♦ tracing paper
♦ spray adhesive
♦ medium-density sponge, such as
a kitchen sponge
♦ scalpel
♦ 3 plates

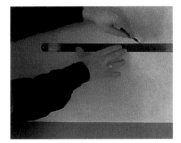

1 Divide the wall by painting the lower section green, up to dado rail height. Measure 24cm/9½in up from the green section and draw a straight line using a pencil, ruler and spirit level to act as a guide for the top of the border.

2 Trace all the pattern shapes, then spray the backs with a light coating of adhesive. Stick them on to the foam and cut out with a scalpel. Press the straight strip into green paint and make a test print. Print a line along the pencil guideline, and another just above the green wall section.

3 Press the curved strip into the green paint, make a test print, then stamp curved lines to form a branch shape.

4 Press the leaf shape into the green paint, make a test print, then stamp them in groups, as shown, two above and one below the branch. ➤

5 Stamp pale pink birds along the branch – you need two prints, one facing each direction. Do not make the prints too uniform; aim for a patchy, textured effect.

6 Clean the sponges, then press them into the crimson paint. Stamp the rest of the birds along the branch, alternating the direction of the motif as before.

7 Stamp a row of pink and crimson hearts above the top line to complete the border pattern.

MINIBUS TOYBOX

Every child should be encouraged to tidy away his or her toys at the end of the day.
This eye-catching toybox might just do the trick!
The pastel-coloured patches behind the bus stamps give the box a 1950s look. These are stencilled on to a
light turquoise background. Stamp the buses on quite randomly so that some extend beyond the background
shapes. Keep changing the angle of the stamp - the effect will be almost three-dimensional.

YOU WILL NEED
- ◆ hinged wooden box
- ◆ emulsion paint in light turquoise
- ◆ paintbrushes
- ◆ pencil
- ◆ ruler
- ◆ sheet of stencil card or mylar
- ◆ spray adhesive
- ◆ scalpel
- ◆ emulsion or stencil paint in yellow, pink and lilac
- ◆ 4 plates
- ◆ small paint roller
- ◆ emulsion or stamping ink in brown
- ◆ rubber roller
- ◆ minibus rubber stamp

1 Apply two coats of turquoise emulsion to the toybox. Leave to dry. Draw and cut out a stencil for the background shape. It should be large enough to contain the whole rubber stamp image with a small border.

2 Spread the three pastel-coloured paints on to separate plates. Using a small roller, paint the first colour through the stencil on to the box. You will need an equal number of shapes for each colour.

3 Wash the roller and apply the two remaining colours, painting through the stencil as before. Balance the shapes with an equal amount of background colour. Leave to dry.

4 Pour some brown emulsion or stamping ink on to a clean plate. Coat the rubber stamp with colour using a rubber roller.

5 Stamp the bus motifs on to the pastel background patches. Allow the stamps to overlap some of the patches and vary the angle of the stamp.

TEMPLATES

The templates on the following pages may be resized to any scale required. They can either be enlarged or reduced on a photocopier, or resized using a grid system. If, for example, a template needs to be enlarged to twice the size shown, copy the design, square by square, onto a grid twice as large as the one provided.

SCANDINAVIAN LIVING-ROOM

PERSONALIZED FLOWERPOTS

SPINNING SUN MOTIF

SUNSTAR WALL

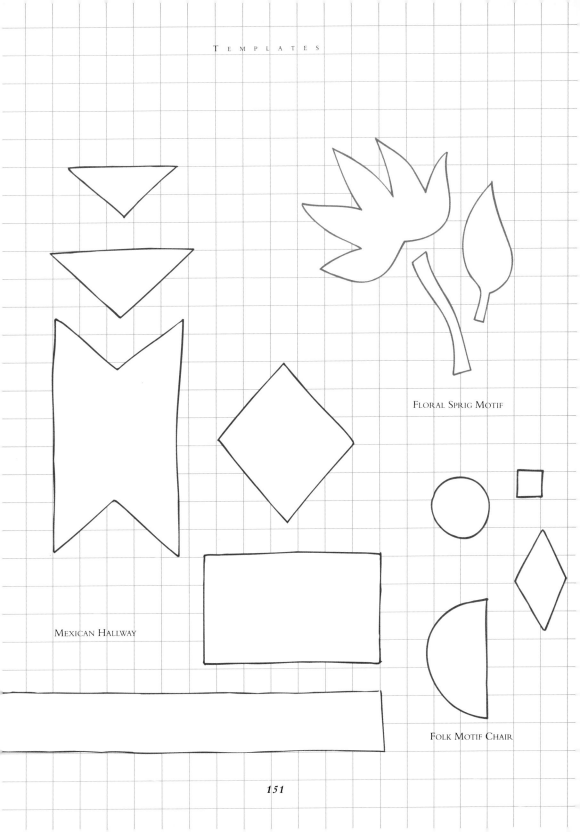

FLORAL SPRIG MOTIF

MEXICAN HALLWAY

FOLK MOTIF CHAIR

CORK-STAMPED FLOORBOARDS

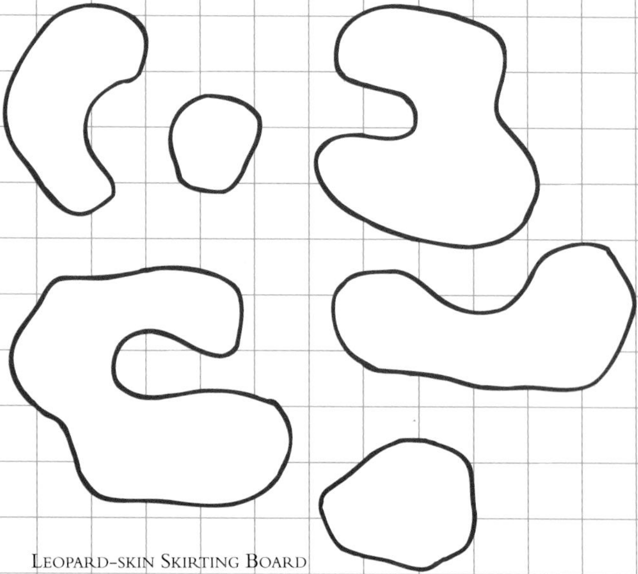

LEOPARD-SKIN SKIRTING BOARD

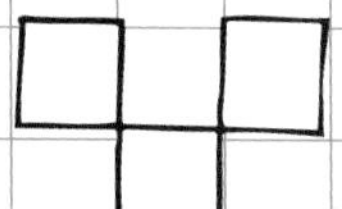

GREEK KEY BATHROOM

COUNTRY-STYLE SHELF

STAR CUPBOARD

FISH FOOTSTOOL

NO-SEW STAR CURTAIN

FLEUR-DE-LIS TILES

SPRIGGED CALICO CURTAINS

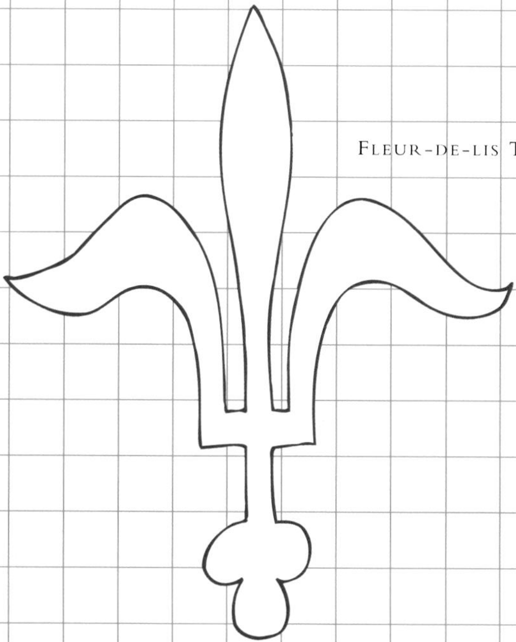

PRIVATE CORRESPONDENCE

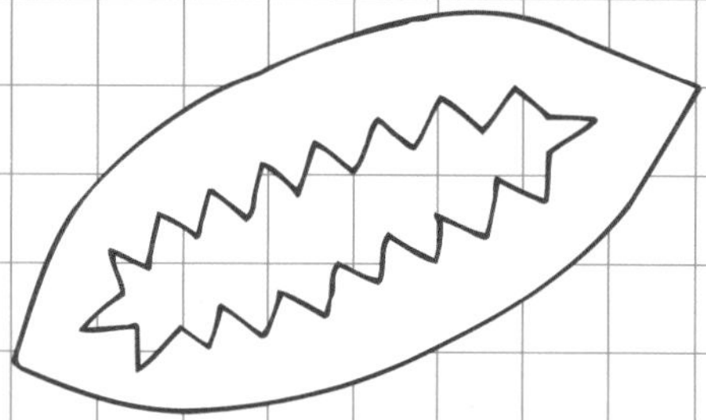

STYLISH LAMPSHADE

STAR-STRUCK TEA SERVICE

SNOWFLAKE STORAGE JARS

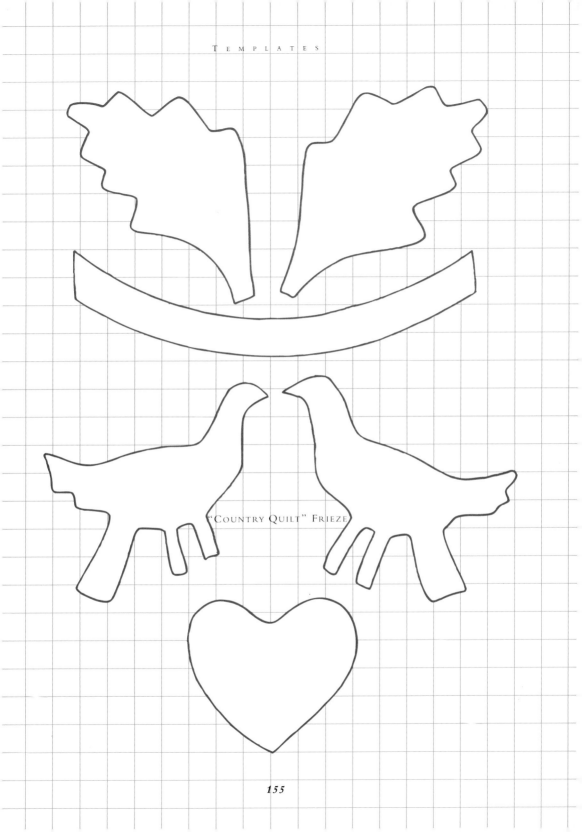

"COUNTRY QUILT" FRIEZE

CARDBOARD GIFT BOX

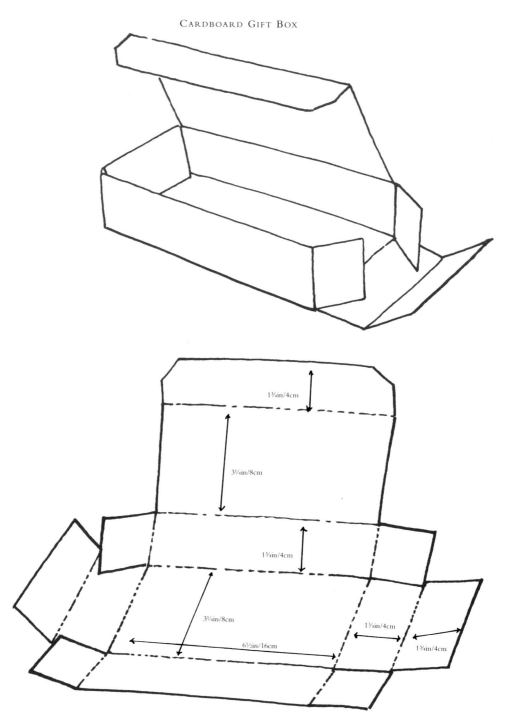

1¾in/4cm

3¼in/8cm

1¾in/4cm

3¼in/8cm

6½in/16cm

1¾in/4cm

1¾in/4cm

STOCKISTS

Annaleey Crafts
P.O. Box 66
Yeelanna SA 5632 Australia
tel: (086) 765 026
fax: (086) 765 014

Art Stamps Australia
354 Military Road
Cremorne NSW 2090 Australia
tel: (02) 9904 1103
fax: (02) 9904 1089

Artarama Stamps
39 Landsdowne Parade
Oatley NSW 2223 Australia
tel: (02) 580 8295
fax: (02) 580 5172

Blade Rubber Stamp Company
2 Neal's Yard
London WC1 England
tel: (0171) 379 7391

Blue Cat Toy Company
Builders Yard
Silver Street
South Cerney
Gloucestershire GL7 4TS England
tel: (01285) 861 867
fax: (01285) 862 153

Early Learning Centre
(Branches country wide, UK)

First Class Stamps Ltd
The Maltings
Hall Staithe, Fakenham
Norfolk NR21 9BW England
tel: (01328) 851 449
fax: (01328) 864 828

Inky Pinky
21 Church Street
Hawthorn Vic 3122 Australia
tel: (03) 9853 3055
fax: (03) 9853 0135

Krafty Lady
No 9, Edgewood Road
Dandenong Vic 3175 Australia
tel/fax: (03) 9794 6064

Print Blocks Pty Ltd
441 Waterworks Road, Ashgrove
Brisbane Qld 4060 Australia
tel: (07) 3366 0366
fax: (07) 3366 0377

Ranger Industries
Tinton Falls
New Jersey 07724 USA

Rubber Stampede
c/o Crafty Ideas
6, The Arcade
Hitchen
Hertfordshire England
tel: (01462) 434 250
fax: (01234) 342 156

The Stamp Connection
14 Edith Road
Faversham
Kent England
ME13 8SD
tel/fax: (01795) 531 860

Stampworld
145 Beattie Street
Balmain NSW 2041 Australia
tel: (02) 818 3111
fax: (02) 818 3388

Woodstock
114 Union Road
Surrey Hills Vic 3127 Australia
tel: (03) 9836 4334
fax: (03) 9836 4226

ACKNOWLEDGEMENTS

The stamps used in the projects in this book are available from the following companies, most of which offer a mail order service (please see Stockists for addresses):

pp 22-3
Sun motif stamp, © Terri McEwen for The Stamp Connection; available direct, or from Blade Rubber Stamp Company.

pp 48-9
Sea motif sponges available from The Early Learning Centre.

pp 50-1
Check border roller, from Rollagraph® by Clearsnap, © Clearsnap Inc; available from Blade Rubber Stamp Company.

pp 77-79; 82-89
Fabric dabber inks, available direct from Ranger Industries, or from the Blue Cat Toy Company.

pp 90-91
Iron-on transfer inks, available direct from Ranger Industries, or from the Blue Cat Toy Company.

pp 96-105
Acrylic enamel and ceramic paints (Liquitex Glossies), distributed by Hinney & Smith, available from good art suppliers nationwide.

pp 147-149
Minibus stamp © Christopher Smith for Blue Cat Toy Company.

All other rubber stamps, stamp ink pads, fabric inks and embossing powders were obtained from The Blue Cat Toy Company.

INDEX

NOTES

NOTES

NOTES

NOTES

NOTES

NOTES

NOTES

NOTES